starting small

starting small

*Teaching Tolerance in Preschool
and the Early Grades*

by Teaching Tolerance
A Project of the Southern Poverty Law Center

TEACHING
TOLERANCE

Teaching Tolerance was founded in 1991 to provide teachers with resources and ideas to help promote harmony in the classroom. The Southern Poverty Law Center is a nonprofit legal and education foundation based in Montgomery, Alabama. The Center's co-founders are Morris S. Dees, Jr., and Joseph J. Levin, Jr. Its directors are Julian Bond, Patricia Clark, Frances Green, Vic Hackley, Howard Mandell and James McElroy.

Project Director
Jim Carnes

Editors
Maria Fleming
Gabrielle Lyon
Ting-Yi Oei
Rosa Hernández Sheets
Glenda Valentine
Elsie Williams

Writers
Sara Bullard
Jim Carnes
Marie Hofer
Nancy Polk
Rosa Hernández Sheets

Design Director
Paul F. Newman

Designer
Rodney Diaz

Illustrator
Yumi Heo

acknowledgments

Grateful acknowledgment is made to the students, parents, teachers and administrators at the following schools: Happy Medium, Seattle, Wash.; Cabrillo College Children's Center, Aptos, Calif.; Maria Mitchell Elementary, Denver, Colo.; Elmwood Elementary, Shawnee, Ohio; Edgewood Elementary, New Haven, Conn.; North Miami Elementary, North Miami, Fla.; State Pre-K Demonstration Center, Chicago, Ill.

Special thanks to Vivian Paley, who contributed the foreword, to Rosa Hernández Sheets for research and commentary, and to Gabrielle Lyon and Maria Fleming for resource reviews. Gratitude also to Eddie Ashworth, Richard Cohen and Erin Kellen for their guidance, and to Margie McGovern, Alex Earl and David Summerlin of Margie McGovern Films, San Francisco, for their invaluable research, patience and vision.

contents

foreword

by Vivian Gussin Paley

The teachers of young children who speak to us so earnestly in the following stories work in different communities but share a common vision: that children can learn to care about every other person's feelings, beliefs and welfare.

The notion may seem commonplace, something surely found in most classrooms. Yet, given the number of sad faces, hurt feelings and lonely outsiders in our schools, the empathy factor may be more talked about than systematically pursued. In the hearts and minds of the teachers described here, it is a full-time commitment that begins anew with each child and family.

The dictionary defines empathy as "understanding so intimate that the feelings, thoughts and motives of one are readily comprehended by another." It is a word often seen on lists of goals but rarely employed as the core curriculum.

Promoting empathy would be a major undertaking for any classroom, but the teachers in this book go further. They believe that perceiving the feelings, thoughts and motives of another person is the first step in building a bridge. What must follow is the discovery, day by day, of how to move — in both directions — *across* that bridge.

Luckily for those who despair of society's ever being made into a kinder place, young children are far more empathetic by nature than we are prone to believe. They are enormously interested in being in the company of other children and are persistently curious about those who seem different. By the time children enter preschool, they are experienced people-watchers, and they know what makes someone laugh or cry.

"Come quick, teacher!" Cynthia calls. "A big boy is crying!"

We follow her to a bench in the hallway where a distraught and dishevelled child is wiping his eyes, embarrassed by our sudden appearance. I recognize him as a 2nd grader who often gets into trouble.

"Martin? What's wrong?" I ask, but the children rush to supply the answers.

"He's lost," says one.

"He wants his mother," says another.

"Someone was mean to him."

"They didn't pay attention. They losed him."

A flicker of a smile crosses Martin's face. He sees that these kindergartners who do not even know him recognize his sense of loss and are ready to befriend and comfort him.

The children *are* ready. They come to school wondering how those so different from themselves can have the same feelings and desires. And we, in turn, must learn how to help them put their intuitive knowledge of commonality into words and actions. This is what children enjoy doing and can do well; it is guaranteed to make our teaching come alive with purpose and meaning.

The teachers we are about to meet also understand that even within a seemingly safe classroom, someone can feel lost and frightened at any moment. They are prepared to stop everything and get everyone to pay attention, to listen to what the other person says and become keenly aware of what to say in response.

In so doing, they give credence to our ultimate goal as teachers in a democratic society: helping children become kind and caring participants in a world that includes everyone. These wise and compassionate teachers who are "starting small" will uncover and model for us the amazingly large moral dimensions of the classroom. ★

introduction

by Jim Carnes

Community begins in the classroom. For most young children, being a "classmate" — at day care, at a place of worship or at school — constitutes their first active participation in an ongoing social structure outside the family. The vision of community that the classroom provides can color a child's ideas and expectations about equity, cooperation and citizenship for a lifetime.

We ask a great deal of children when they enter the classroom: to leave the familiar environment of home; to encounter peers and adults who may look, act, speak and think differently from themselves and their family; and to "fit in" successfully with these strangers as learners and friends. Although such tasks involve unique developmental dimensions in young children, public life presents all of us with a similar challenge. The capacity to thrive in diversity is a lifelong practice of discovery and adaptation, as new differences unfailingly arise. More and more early childhood teachers have come to recognize that teaching tolerance outright in the curriculum is as fundamental and as far-reaching as teaching children how to read.

Such an endeavor raises serious questions: How can teachers acquire the necessary skills and tools? What kind of peer, administrative, parental and community support do they need? How are they supposed to add "tolerance" or "multicultural-ism" or "character education" to an already overcrowded curriculum? The real challenge, perhaps, is less a matter of expanding the job than of re-imagining it. What follows is a close look at a number of individual and team teachers whose effectiveness derives not from extraordinary talents, conditions or resources but from extraordinary visions of possibility in an imperfect world.

This book profiles seven classrooms in which teachers are helping young children build inclusive, equitable, caring communities across differences that too often divide. Their approaches are as varied as their faces and names, yet they share three crucial habits: *reflecting* continually on their own assumptions, goals and behavior; *talking* with their peers about how these factors conflict as well as coincide; and *practicing* social skills as diligently as mental or physical ones.

In a Chicago housing project, you will meet a school director who struggles with what it means to be a White teacher of Black children. At Sharing Time in a Seattle primary class, you will find children comfortable enough to voice their deepest concerns. And you will visit a Denver school in which practicing simple hospitality helps kindergartners become citizens of the world. In myriad ways, these classrooms demonstrate that lofty ideals like tolerance, justice and peace often begin as child's play.

During the lengthy process of identifying some 300 ground-breaking early childhood educators across the country, we encountered many we regret to omit from these pages. Our aim for variety in geographical distribution, school setting, student population, curriculum content and teaching style led us to the exemplary group presented here.

This book has seven chapters, each centered on an in-depth classroom narrative. Two kinds of sidebars supplement the main stories. "Reflections" are research-based essays addressing specific themes or developmental aspects of teaching tolerance, such as racial awareness, gender equity or friendship. "Applications" offer practical ideas for incorporating these concepts into classroom activities. It is important to acknowledge the inherent overlap among many aspects of diversity that we have chosen to highlight. Our intention is to treat these as complementary themes rather than as independent constructs. In addition to the sidebars, an extensive annotated resource list surveys the best materials available — both comprehensive and specialized — in the field of early childhood diversity education.

Tolerance, justice and peace *are* lofty ideals. Most adults find them difficult to realize. For capable and confident teachers at any level, the goal of dispelling stereotypes and prejudice, fostering respect for differences and building community in the classroom can be a daunting one. At first glance, it would seem an especially tall order for a classroom of young children. But, as the teachers in this book affirm, everything is easier when you start small. ★

seattle, washington

everybody's story

I n the bustling hallway outside her classroom, Debra Goldsbury reminds her students to hang their coats on the hooks, to sign in and take their places on the rug for Sharing Time. April's great-grandparents have brought her to school today. Devon is wearing a red velvet jester's hat his mom made. Debra notices that Abigail isn't her usual smiling self this morning. She calls the diminutive 6-year-old aside and rests a hand on her shoulder.

"I'm sad," Abigail says without prompting. Her big brown eyes are lusterless.

"I can tell," Debra says. She bends closer, her face mirroring the child's sorrow. "Do you want to talk about it?"

Today, Abigail explains, her birth mom is leaving Seattle. Although Abigail lived in a foster home for two years and recently moved in with a family who are preparing to adopt her, she has continued to visit her birth mother often. Now, that will change. Just telling someone about this allows her face to brighten a little.

A sign on the bulletin board in Debra's mixed-age primary classroom reads, "Let's talk. Let's all talk. What we don't talk about hurts us all."

It's an idea that informs every aspect of life at Happy Medium School, located a few blocks west of downtown Seattle. (The name derives from the school's motto: "Children thrive in a happy medium.") At Sharing Time, first thing in the morning, each child gets a turn to bring up whatever's on his or her mind. Sebastian reports, "My mom's friend, Curt, is going to the mountains with us. I may be getting a stepdad!"

"On the way to school this morning," announces Bonnie, "I found an old shoe."

Abigail stands up to show off her new sweatshirt, printed with a family photograph. "Is that your foster family?" someone asks, and she nods solemnly.

Around the circle sit 14 children, as varicolored as pebbles. The visible diversity among students at Happy Medium is central to the school's philosophy. But just as important, says Debra Goldsbury, who is White, is the invisible diversity that our society often fails to understand, affirm or even acknowledge. Two children in her room, for example, come from homes with two moms. Several have single parents. Four members of the class are adopted.

School director Susan Kerr, herself a White adoptive parent in an interracial family, has devoted her life to studying how families are built. "There are teachers who still say, 'Do a family tree,' which is impossible for many children." A few years ago, a teacher on Kerr's staff asked students to copy the information on their birth certificates, including the little footprints. Half of the children were adopted and did not have access to their original certificates.

Kerr would like to make educators more conscious of family

diversity, "so that it becomes a natural thought, instead of a 'special' thought. I cannot presume that you grew up with your mother and father. If I ask you, 'What was your best childhood memory of your grandma, or your dad?' you may not have any memories at all. We need to be more open-ended in how we talk about these things."

The admissions policy at Happy Medium is "first come, first served," with special considerations for maintaining schoolwide racial and gender balance. The staff's interest in family diversity has made the school popular with adoptive, interracial, and gay and lesbian parents. Kerr points out emphatically that there is no admissions testing, academic or otherwise. Several students' families receive assistance from the Department of Human Services. Three children in Debra's class have parents who work at the school in lieu of paying tuition.

Debra finds that encouraging open discussion of home life — both its joys and its sorrows — fosters empathy among her students. Devon is a biracial child who moved to Seattle with his mother in the fall after his father deserted them in California. One morning at Sharing Time, Devon said that his mom had had a fight with her sister the night before, which meant that he would "never ever" see his favorite cousin again.

Later in the day, Devon "just went off," says Debra. "He started yelling at another kid, when he's ordinarily the world's caretaker." Knowing the story behind the behavior, she was able to pull him aside and say, "I'm so sorry you're having a bad day." He fell against her and sobbed.

Abigail, who knew the story, too, came over to him and said, "Sometimes I miss my foster family so much my throat hurts. Does your throat hurt?"

In a faint, squeaky voice, Devon said, "Yes." Spontaneously, the nearby children enveloped him in a big group hug.

A school environment where family diversity is a given allows children to see beyond their differences to their common concerns. Kim Buchanan, who teaches pre-kindergarten across the hall from Debra's room, explains: "I have several interracial children in my class. Kids with single moms. I have one child living with his grandma, where Mom floats in and out. One child's father committed suicide, and she's very much aware of it. But no one in the room is worried about whether these are 'traditional' families or not."

In Debra Goldsbury's view, "What children are really concerned about is that there *is* a family, that there are people who love them. What frightens them is the idea of being totally alone, of having no one."

This year, Debra has one boy whose mother is a foster parent to other children. A succession of temporary siblings have shared his home all his life. This child's experience on the "other side" of the family-building process has made him a natural ally of Abigail and the other adoptees.

Sharing Time

"I think children have amazing respect for each other's stories," says Debra, who decided to switch careers from community activism to teaching 9 years ago, after she began volunteering in her son's kindergarten classroom.

She considers Sharing Time the most important activity of the day. "Over the years, I've tried a lot of different ways to begin the day, but I find if I let them share first thing in the morning, I can almost always count on cooperation for the rest of the day. If for some reason we don't have Sharing for several days in a row, it just comes out on its own."

Only four topics are off-limits for Sharing in Debra's room: brand-name toys, movies, video games and TV. Once the Power

Rangers and *Jurassic Park* were banished from the circle, she explains, the kids tuned in to their real thoughts, feelings and activities.

Kim Buchanan believes that "in most school situations, kids come to school able to talk, and we immediately shut them up. In the traditional classroom, the first thing that goes is their voice. We want them to write, we want them to read, but we don't want them to talk."

One of the things that Debra and her class talk about often is safety — not just the "fire and traffic" kind, but emotional safety, the sense of well-being that can exist only where there is respect and trust. "We spend the whole first month just talking about what makes a person feel safe or unsafe. Put-downs, name-calling — these are things that violate safety."

Recently, Debra's students collected canned foods to donate to the community food bank, located near the school. One child commented that "those people at food banks are lazy and don't work," and Debra paused to correct him. But another class member spoke up first: "When my mom lost her job, we had to go to a food bank for a while." Suddenly, "those people" became real, and a stereotype faded.

Loss is a theme that Susan Kerr finds increasingly common in the lives of young children — loss of economic security, loss of physical and emotional protection, loss of a parent or of the family structure itself. In conjunction with the Children's Home Society of Seattle, she received a Kellogg Grant to develop a curriculum that takes into account these "complex life experiences," as the project terms them.

Children moving into foster care, Kerr points out, sometimes take with them only what fits into a suitcase. "They may never again smell the smell of what's familiar to them. They may never again hear the sound of what's familiar.

"They lose that connection, they may never get it back, and there's no one to talk with them about it. And yet we're asking them to be delightful, energetic, well-behaved, prepared to learn. So when we talk to educators, we try to remind them of this, not to create a sense of drama but a sense of awareness that those losses are meaningful. That they're not just something you put behind you and go on."

Earlier this year, a 5-year-old White boy enrolled at Happy Medium shortly after being placed in foster care, awaiting termination of parental rights. He was assigned to a classroom with two teachers, one Black and one White.

According to Kerr, "He came to school out of this chaos and attached — I mean literally *attached* — to this young African American teacher." During an activity involving mixing paint to make handprints in the children's skin colors, the boy printed one hand using the beige or "White" paint and the other using dark brown. The teacher asked him which was his handprint. "This one," he said, pointing to the lighter color. "*And* this one. I'm really like you."

"When we talk about attachment and trust," Kerr observes, "here was this little White boy losing his family and identifying with his Black teacher. He's not in denial about what color he is, but he's saying, 'I belong with you.' We did it again three months later and he did both of his handprints 'White.' Then he went over to the teacher and said, 'You know, I'm still like you.'

"These kids are dealing with amazingly complex stuff," says Kerr. "The issue is whether we as adults are comfortable enough and aware enough to deal with it."

Happy Medium teachers agree that no magic line divides school life from family life. They believe that school is, in fact, a part of each student's extended family. Whatever is happening at home — whether trivial or terrifying — is a legitimate topic for classroom discussion.

Three years ago, Debra Goldsbury had seven children in her class, six of whom were facing the death or terminal illness of a loved one. Inga's father was dying of AIDS. Her parents had told her as plainly as they could what the disease was and how it was going to change their family. She tried to be a brave 6-year-old. Sometimes she even went with her dad when he gave talks to groups of people about living with AIDS. But whenever she got scared or sad, she went to a secret place she called Thursberg.

As her father's condition worsened, Inga's parents' friends in the Seattle arts community rallied around the family. They tried to give Inga plenty of fun things to do to keep her mind off her worries. Inga's classmates knew about the illness, though she hardly ever mentioned it at Sharing Time. They also knew she went to "Thursberg" a lot, but she never described it to anyone. Inga had always been quiet and solitary at school. She told her teacher that kids were boring — she'd rather play with adults.

One day Debra asked the class for ideas for a bulletin-board mural they could make. Several suggestions came up before Inga raised her hand. She proposed making a mural of Thursberg.

"I think she just needed to have people share a part of her life that was beautiful," says Debra. "It was difficult for her in some ways because she had very clear ideas of what it was going to be, and she had to let go of some of those. She shared it, so it was very beautiful to watch."

Three years after its creation, the bright collage still occupies most of one wall in the school office. In Thursberg there are no cars — the people ride dinosaurs. The sun is a heart in a rainbow sky, and all the clouds are shaped like animals. Pink grass grows beside a red Jello river. Your house can be whatever you want: One person's is a pyramid, another's a turreted castle. Everyone works in a job they like.

In the process of sharing ideas and representing them on

paper, the class created its own utopian community. And Inga wasn't the only one who found an outlet for her fears.

During one mural work session, Inga said she wished that her father could live until she was 12, although she didn't think he would even live until she was 8. Judith, another little girl in the room, had a terminally ill mother but didn't want anyone besides the teacher to know. Debra saw Judith with her head down and then noticed that the child's dress front was soaked with tears.

Judith looked up and said, "My mom's going to die, too." For the first time, as everyone listened, she began to tell her story.

Kids Belong Together

In an era when many private primary schools encourage intense academic competitiveness, Happy Medium emphasizes interactive learning through play. "We tell prospective parents right up front that if they want their children to accelerate or become computer geniuses, and to be reading and writing at four, then don't bring them here," explains Susan Kerr.

Instead, she describes her program in terms of values: "We want our children to understand the meaning of compassion and fairness and resolving problems without beating on each other. We want them to understand how they belong and who belongs and how everyone's connected."

When discussing diversity issues with students and parents alike, Debra Goldsbury believes in "cutting to the chase." She asks parents who are considering sending their children to Happy Medium, "Who is your child's peer group?" Her own conviction is clear: "*This* is their peer group — this multiculturalism is real. This is who they'll be spending their time with, hiring, marrying. No matter where they are."

Small visual details throughout the building contribute to an environment of pluralism. A hallway bulletin board features a sequence of photocopied hands spelling "Kim's Class" in sign language. The clock in the school office has Japanese numerals. A framed piece of Hmong needlework hangs over the assistant director's desk. The "Thursberg" mural dominates one wall, opposite an embroidered image of colorful winged children taking flight. Nearby, a calendar proclaims the unofficial Happy Medium motto: "Let's talk. Let's all talk. ..."

Teachers infuse diversity into all areas of the curriculum. Virtually any subject, from dancing to dinosaurs, offers opportunities for discussing similarity and difference. A citywide project to make quilts for children with AIDS has given rise in Debra's room to a multicultural exploration of quilts, blankets and the whole idea of comfort.

"At this age," Debra points out, "many children have a favorite blanket. And all cultures use quilts or blankets somehow. There are so many natural connections."

One of the teacher's most important tasks, as Debra sees it, is simply to keep the discussion flowing. Recently, Shantha's mother brought their household altar in and told the class about Krishna and Kali and the other gods and goddesses worshipped by the Nepali Hindu family. Rodrigo, a Latino child of the Catholic faith, said, "My mom said you don't believe in Jesus."

Shantha's mother described her tradition's inclusive theology. "We love Jesus," she said. "Jesus was a wonderful wise person."

Her statement satisfied Rodrigo, but Tommy, whose African American family is devoutly Baptist, was more skeptical. "Do you go to church on Sunday?" he asked.

"No, we don't," said the visitor. "We worship in other ways, every day. We have this altar in our house."

Debra saw Tommy struggling to accept this answer. When she asked him how he felt about what he had just heard, he paused, then grinned and said, "That's Shantha!"

The flash of Tommy's smile signaled for Debra Goldsbury the kind of small insight a teacher hopes for. "What an awareness!" she says. "That this isn't just some odd person doing this. 'This is my friend Shantha, whose family does this. And she eats a peanut butter sandwich every day just like I do.'"

Over the past eight years, family, racial and religious diversity have been woven into the Happy Medium fabric. But other differences remain at issue among parents and staff. A current challenge concerns students with behavior problems. Susan Kerr remains skeptical of programs that segregate "problem" children from their peers.

"There are new ways of working with certain kids," she asserts, "without having to call them Attention Deficit Disordered or Attachment Disordered or Hyperactive. We can say, 'They come from a complex life experience.' They're still our kids. They belong here."

Occasionally, the parent-teacher board must grapple with questions of how well a child's special needs are being served by the school or whether the situation is monopolizing the teacher's time. So far, no behavior issue has caused a child to be removed from or denied admission to Happy Medium.

Debra admits, "It's a fine line we're walking. Yes, we want to be inclusive. I tell parents that one of the life skills children need is how to deal with difficult children. But there are limits to what is fair to everyone."

Another challenge facing the school is the inclusion of mobility-impaired students. While children with a variety of disabilities — deafness, blindness, cerebral palsy — have attended Happy Medium, the present facility does not accommodate wheelchairs. Long-range plans for a new building, Kerr says, will address this need.

"I want kids to come who have all kinds of issues," she adds.

"Kids belong together. Out in the world, they're going to be side by side, so this is a good place to practice."

A Million and Nine Colors

It's late March, but Debra Goldsbury is showing her class a group photograph from the beginning of the school year. "Why don't we have this picture on the wall any more?" she asks her 14 students.

"Because there were only eight of us," says Martin.

"Now we have more," Emily adds. Other voices join in to name Daniel, Abigail, Sebastian, April, Devon and Bonnie, all second-semester arrivals.

"I would like for this to be the best year ever," Debra tells the class. "Have you noticed anything different lately, besides the fact that we're bigger? Have you noticed any problems?"

As Debra has predicted, the class is quick to cite several: The teacher has to raise her voice more often. There's been a lot of hitting and fighting. Kids are paying less attention to the rules they made as a group at the beginning of the year.

The class Constitution hangs on the front wall. The original eight children drafted it by consensus back in September, and Goldsbury inscribed it on poster board, complete with "antiqued" edges. It has occurred to her recently that that document may be part of the problem.

Since January, her class has nearly doubled in size. The new students have no ownership in the agreements the previous children created. As she puts it, "We haven't done anything to include the new group, to create a new identity with this whole class."

At today's meeting they decide to start over, from scratch: Take everything off the walls, create new self-portraits, abolish the old Constitution and adopt a new one. The students who had been there from the beginning would become teachers — reinforcing their own understanding of community by helping their new classmates take part.

"It's going to be interesting to see how it will go at mid-year," she says. "It's an experiment. I'm sticking my neck out here. I can anticipate some of the things they might do, but I'm asking young children to do a task that's even difficult for adults, which is to include somebody new."

The walls of the room are bare. One of the activities Debra always opens the year with is painting self-portraits with People Colors — one of several commercial lines of "multicultural" paints and crayons. Today, she invites each new child, in turn, to find the paint mixture that matches his or her skin tone. The old-timers have been using these colors for months now.

"I'm gingerbread," says Rodrigo.

"I'm melon and terra cotta," boasts Millie.

"Raise your hand," Debra says, "if your color is close to Millie's." April volunteers.

"April's a little darker than Millie," someone comments.

"Do you think that's because April just moved here from California and has more of a suntan?" Debra inquires. She fingers a streak of melon onto April's hand — too pale — then mixes in some terra cotta.

"I can't even see it," Sebastian says when April shows the smudge around.

"So what does that mean," Debra asks, "if you can't see the paint I just put on her skin?"

"It's a match!" cries Martin.

Debra calls Daniel, one of the new children, to the front.

"I'm White," he says.

"Nobody's white," says Tommy.

Daniel's face falls.

Right there, as Debra hears it, is the whole new kid/old kid issue in two short sentences. At Daniel's previous school, no one ever suggested that society's color coding could be questioned. "What happens," Debra asks the class, "when Daniel says 'I'm White,' and we say 'Nobody's white'?"

"He doesn't feel good," says LaKecia.

"I mean he's not white like *these*," Tommy explains, pointing to his own athletic socks.

Debra takes Daniel's hand. "One of the things we decided back in the fall," she tells him, "was that instead of saying we're white or black or brown we'd find out exactly what color we are. We start with these 12 colors the factory makes, and then we mix and match. How many colors of children do you think there are in the world?"

"A million and nine," says Daniel with a shrug. After sampling several People Colors on the back of his hand and displaying them around the circle, he grins and announces, "I'm peach!"

In Debra's view, exercises like self-portraiture that explore and validate individual traits and perceptions help to orient young children in their social sphere. A clear sense of their own physical and emotional identity permits them to regard their peers as unique equals. After the paint has dried, Debra groups the fresh faces on a bulletin board to form a new class portrait.

Unity in Community

Piece by piece, the room is coming together. On the bare front wall, Debra hangs a poster she has made of some proverbs inscribed on the steps of the nearby community center: "Welcome unity in the community." "Peace cannot be kept by force. It can only be achieved through understanding." "It takes a whole village to raise a child." "Let's talk. Let's all talk. What we don't talk about hurts us all."

Next to it she places a large sheet of paper labeled "Community Constitution," with two blank columns for the rights and responsibilities the class will vote to adopt. She repeats a question she first asked seven months ago: "What rights do we all have as members of the community in this room?"

A flock of small hands takes to the air. "The right to learn!" "To play!" "We have the right to have things." Debra records each suggestion on the left-hand column, reminding the class that every right brings a responsibility.

"We all have the right to learn, so we all have the responsibility to ..."

"Teach!"

"That's good," Debra says. "We all teach each other, as well as learn from each other. I'm not the only teacher in this room, and you aren't the only learners."

Other examples fill out the page: The right to play brings the responsibility to cooperate and play fairly. The right to have things brings the responsibility to share. As Debra notices the newer kids joining the others in this exercise, she sees the distinctions of new and old disappearing. At recess time she will take the document out to the playground and ceremonially burn its edges, to give it the earmark of history.

"It feels good to regroup, doesn't it?" Debra says. "I think we should celebrate! Communities need to celebrate their togetherness." She opens the floor for ideas.

Devon suggests that the boys make a paper chain and the girls make whatever they want to decorate the room.

Millie says she doesn't like that idea.

"Why not?" Debra asks.

"Because it wouldn't show we're all together."

Someone else proposes a tea party.

"What kind of tea party could we have?" asks Debra.

"A doll tea party!"

"A stuffed animal tea party."

Rodrigo is staring intently at his new track shoes. "I have an idea," he says. His face lights up. "A new shoe tea party!" Then his eyes narrow again as he stretches the thought: "How about a new shoe/old shoe tea party? That includes everyone. Even the girls, because they wear shoes, too!"

The next day, Debra brings a box to school containing a china teapot, linen napkins, herbal tea and cookies. At Sharing Time that morning, she picks up Rodrigo's theme.

"Stick your feet out, everyone, so we can see your shoes. Let's talk about how shoes are the same and how they're different."

Devon goes first: "Abigail's and Rodrigo's and mine are Converses."

"Is that the same or different?" asks Debra.

"Same!"

Millie says, "They all protect our feet. That's the same."

"Some are old and some are new."

"Different!" chimes the circle.

"We all wear them," says Shantha.

"Same!"

"Some have laces and some have buckles."

"Different!"

"My shoes and Rodrigo's and Tommy's shoes are high-tops," says Martin, "but Daniel's and Shantha's aren't."

"Different!"

"That's the same *and* different," Millie observes.

Each child in turn puts a new spin on the concept: They keep our feet clean. Some have stripes. Mine are cloth, yours are leather.

Debra scans the circle of sneakers, sandals, scuffed boots, polished slippers. Different and the same, they form the outline of a world. ★

16

R E F L E C T I O N   I

Racial and Ethnic Awareness

Identity — an understanding of who we are and who we are not — is a complex, multifaceted process that begins in childhood and continues throughout life. Early in their identity development, children become aware of a wide range of physical characteristics in themselves and others, including those we call racial — skin color, facial features, hair texture. Likewise, young children acquire ethnic values, customs, language styles and behavioral codes long before they are able to label and know them as ethnic. Much later, in middle childhood, they begin to understand the cultural and political dimensions of race and ethnicity and the significant role these factors play in their lives.

Numerous studies from a cognitive developmental perspective show that infants and preschoolers notice racial cues. In one study conducted in a Chinese hospital, Chinese infants reacted more negatively to White strangers than to Chinese strangers; when U.S. children ages 3 to 4 were shown photos of three people and asked to match the two that "go together," skin color was the determinant used most often (Ramsey, 1986).

Racial Language

As children develop race awareness, they acquire racial language to describe and categorize self and others. Children adapt their own words for this purpose, as well as apply existing racial vocabulary they hear from peers and adults. Conceptual inconsistencies between these two sets of terms are often reflected in children's usage. To illustrate: 3-year-old Cecilia picks up a brown crayon to draw a picture of her friend Kira. She says that both the crayon and her friend are "black." Cecilia also calls a black crayon "black" but will not use it to color her "black" friend.

Robyn Holmes (1995) found that 5-year-old White children often use the word "white" to describe their own skin color, even though they use crayons in varying shades from pink to light brown to color self-portraits. Her research indicated that 5-year-old Black children tended not to use the word "black" to describe themselves. When Holmes asked Maureen, "What do you think it means when somebody says 'You're black'?" she answered, "People call me black, but I'm not. I'm really brown." Black children in this study described Black people as having varying shades of brown skin.

Around age 5, children can typically describe a range of physical characteristics using a mixture of race/color terms such as "black," "white" and "brown" and generalized ethnic designations such as "Japanese," "Chinese" and "Spanish." In one study, children ages 3 to 5 from a variety of racial groups categorized people as "Chinese" or "Japanese" on the basis of eye shape and skin color (Ramsey, 1986). This expansion of vocabulary, even when it leads to inaccuracy, indicates a growing recognition of racial and ethnic complexities. It also shows that young children can perceive and describe physical differences associated with race before they are able to understand that these attributes can categorize people as members of a specific racial and/or ethnic group.

Racial-Ethnic Identity

Scholars who study racial and ethnic development in young children from a socialization perspective believe that the ethnic identity process for children of color begins at birth — at the earliest interactions between the child, family and community (Cross & Fhagen-Smith, 1996; Spencer, 1985). They maintain that the continual presence of personal and societal markers — skin color, language, food choices, values, and membership in a dominant or non-dominant group — instills in children ethnic roles and behaviors that prepare them for eventual self-labeling.

Racially mixed children also follow a sequential pattern of color differentiation, racial awareness and self-labeling. Studies show that multiracial children develop racial awareness earlier than White children and later than their Black peers, but by ages 3 and 4 most multiracial children are aware of racial differences (Johnson, in Root, 1992).

However, self-labeling can be problematic for multiracial children. It is difficult for young children to explain that they have a dual or more complex heritage while societal norms often force them to identify and affiliate with a single racial or ethnic group. Additionally, multiracial identity scholars assert that even at a young age multiracial children can sense social conflict among racial groups (Johnson, in Root, 1992). For example, a young biracial child, perceived as Black, can sense the teacher's discomfort and his peers' surprise at seeing his White mother. Although terms such as "biracial," "multiracial" and "mixed race" are often used by multiracial families, some biracial children continually face out-of-home experiences that do not support the development of dual-race identity.

The prominence of so-called racial attributes in young children's perception of diversity helps explain why race is such a confounding concept in our society. While racial categories involve a range of biological traits, race itself is not a biological phenomenon — there is no "race gene." Yet the conventional categories of race reflect differences that even infants can perceive. To minimize for young people the reality of these physical differences — "In our room, we don't see color" — can be as harmful as ignoring the social and political implications of race.

Most studies of racial awareness in young children have focused on Asian, Black and White populations. Further research is needed to help us understand how all children make distinctions among racially and ethnically diverse people. While such issues are sensitive for adults, children speak candidly about their observations and feelings concerning differences. To understand how racism, prejudice and discrimination develop, we must begin by examining race and ethnicity through children's eyes (see Prejudice Formation, p. 99).

References

Cross, W. E., & Fhagen-Smith, P. (1996). "Nigrescence and Ego Identity Development: Accounting for Differential Black Identity Patterns." In P. B. Pederson, J. G. Draguns, W. J. Lonner, & J. E. Trimble (Eds.), Counseling Across Cultures (4th ed., pp. 108-123). Thousand Oaks, CA: Sage.

Holmes, R. M. (1995). How Young Children Perceive Race. Thousand Oaks, CA: Sage.

Ramsey, P. G. (1986). "Racial and Cultural Categories." In C. P. Edwards (Ed.), Promoting Social and Moral Development in Young Children: Creative Approaches for the Classroom (pp. 78-101). New York: Teachers College Press.

Root, M. P. P. (Ed.). (1992). Racially Mixed People in America. Thousand Oaks, CA: Sage.

Spencer, M. (1985). "Cultural Cognition and Social Cognition as Identity Factors in Black Children's Personal Growth." In M. Spencer, G. Brookins, & W. Allen (Eds.), Beginnings: The Social and Affective Development of Black Children (pp. 215-230). Hillsdale, NJ: Lawrence Erlbaum.

20

Affirming Identity

Through their own perceptions and the messages of others, young children construct an understanding of race and ethnicity that significantly shapes their self-image and, by extension, their behavior and relationships. The following activities are designed to assist in promoting children's racial-ethnic identity development. Evidence of self-respect and positive interaction with diverse peers and caregivers can serve as an evaluation tool.

- Encourage children to notice and appreciate their own physical traits and those of others. For example:
  1 Provide hand-held mirrors to let children inspect their own faces and a large mirror at child level so they can see themselves full-size with their friends.
  2 Throughout the year, engage children in self-portrait activities in a variety of media (e.g., "People Colors," collage, clay). In some of the activities, emphasize careful attention to skin color, hair texture and facial features.
  3 Make "Who Am I?" snapshots of children's hands or the backs of their heads. Have a guessing game for identifying the photos, then display them as an alternative class portrait.

- Examine the curriculum and classroom climate for indirect messages about race and ethnicity. For example:
  1 Include materials in shades of brown and black in your room decorations and art projects.
  2 In storybooks, watch for patterns of association between

light- or dark-colored characters and positive or negative traits.

3 In addition to encouraging cross-cultural interaction, allow children of all races and languages to use same-race, same-language interactions as a personal resource.

■ Create opportunities for children and staff to process racially and ethnically related information. For example:

1 Affirm children's curiosity about their own or others' race or ethnicity (e.g., if 3-year old Jade, a Filipina, asks "I'm Pino-Pino, right?" say "Yes" and point out relevant special facts, such as the ability to speak two languages, beautiful skin color or unique cultural traditions).

2 Use materials and lessons that honor the contributions, values and heritages of diverse peoples.

3 Lead discussions and activities that openly value racial and ethnic diversity in the classroom (e.g., compare and contrast skin colors and affirm the beauty of all of them; explain that children usually — but not always — have physical traits similar to those of their family members).

4 If children express confusion about race/color terms, acknowledge that although "Black" and "White" refer to racial categories they are not accurate descriptions of skin color. Point out that people come in many shades.

5 Discuss with friends and colleagues from different backgrounds how they first became aware of their racial and/or ethnic identity.

6 Provide positive role models by encouraging and recruiting teachers of diverse racial and ethnic backgrounds to work in your school.

R E F L E C T I O N 2

Family Diversity

Every child is a member of a family. Regardless of where or with whom children live, they belong to a group of people who share one or more of the following family ties: kinship, affection, cultural knowledge and resources. While the term "family diversity" is often used to describe racial and ethnic variations, other factors, such as adoption, foster care, socioeconomic status and lifestyle, also account for differences among families. These factors in themselves do not determine the amount nor the quality of nurturing young children receive. All kinds of families can provide the love and support necessary for healthy psychosocial development.

Myths and stereotypes about the "ideal" family can influence teacher expectations and attitudes regarding the ability of children to learn and behave. Some homes may be consciously or subconsciously judged unsatisfactory or culturally inferior simply on the basis of race, lifestyle, family structure or socioeconomic status. By acknowledging and celebrating a wide spectrum of families in the curriculum, early childhood teachers can discourage prejudgment and reinforce the vital link between home and school.

Family relationships and child-rearing practices exert a fundamental influence on identity development. Families create, or fail to create, children's earliest sense of belonging, uniqueness and competence. Generally speaking, parents' race, ethnicity, language, religion and other cultural attributes determine those of the child. However, adoption, foster care, extensive child-care services and diverse family structures may introduce racial and cultural differences among family members.

Research shows that one in four children under the age of 6 lives in a family that is below the national poverty level (National Center for Children in Poverty, 1996). Children from economically distressed families endure conditions, such as inadequate shelter, inferior food and unsafe neighborhoods, that affect their emotional, social and educational well-being. Often it is not the lack of income per se but the presence of stress in the home environment that accounts for the negative adjustment of children (Graham-Bermann, 1996). Disruptions and traumas in children's lives are associated with increased social and behavioral problems. For some of these children, teachers and classmates are a primary source of continuity and social-emotional support *(see* Childhood Losses, *p. 189).*

Language Differences

At a very young age, children are required to negotiate difficult transitions between home and school. While it is challenging for any child to enter a new environment, this experience can be terrifying for young children whose home language differs from that of the classroom. Approximately 31.8 million residents of the United States — more than one in seven — speak a language other than English as their primary language (U.S. Census Bureau, 1990). Contrary to popular belief, most U.S. schoolchildren from non-English-speaking families are native-born citizens.

In the classroom, linguistic isolation can make children feel unsafe, unimportant and friendless. These psychological and social factors sometimes outweigh the cognitive challenges of learning a new language. Researcher Cristina Igoa (1995) observed the drawings of immigrant children and saw baby birds falling out of trees, fish swimming on sidewalks and other scenes expressing what she interprets as feelings of fear, lone-liness, fatigue and rootlessness. Igoa believes that the psycho-logical and cultural trauma immigrant children experience is often obscured by the fact that most of them eventually learn to speak English.

The issue of language differences between home and school also affects many children who speak English but come from cultural backgrounds outside the mainstream. Children from Appalachia or other regions with distinct speech pat-terns, for example, or children who speak Black English may encounter communication barriers in the classroom.

To be successful with diverse linguistic groups, teachers must acknowledge the functions of language beyond direct exchange of information. Every language embodies both the historical experience of a particular cultural group and the conscious effort by that group to transmit its collective values (Vygotsky, 1962). Native speakers of a given language utilize not only its grammar and vocabulary but also its distinctive verbal customs and patterns of thought, which help to shape styles of learning.

For example, the turn-taking, eye contact and conversational sequence observed in many U.S. schools may be foreign to some children in a diverse classroom. A child from a culture that values spontaneous and exuberant call-and-response group dialogue, for example, may have difficulty raising her hand and waiting to be called on. Conversely, a child from a culture in which personal opinion and emotion are considered inap-propriate for public display may withdraw from class participa-tion (Minami & McCabe, 1995). In addition to these broader cultural factors, teachers should bear in mind that many young children are in transition from the casual communication style used at home to the more formal one of school and society.

Cultural Values

Another element of family life that many young children bring into the classroom is a framework of cultural knowledge and values grounded in religious tradition. The challenge for teachers is simultaneously to affirm this aspect of cultural identity, to help children recognize and appreciate religious diversity, and to avoid promoting a particular religion. Some teachers meet these goals by allowing children to "share" religious traditions in the larger context of "What we do in my family." Sensitivity to these issues will ensure that every child's religious beliefs and practices — or lack thereof — receive equal respect and accommodation.

Teachers can observe children's behaviors in order to identify and assess the learning preferences, cognitive strengths and cultural values that originate in the home. This child-generated knowledge is an essential component of an equitable curriculum. In turn, such information opens doors for more meaningful interaction with parents and other caregivers. *(See also Racial and Ethnic Awareness, p. 16.)*

References

Graham-Bermann, S. A., Coupet, S., Egler, L., Mattis, J., & Banyard, V. (1996). "Interpersonal Relationships and Adjustment of Children in Homeless and Economically Distressed Families." *Journal of Clinical Child Psychology,* 25 (3) 250-261.

Igoa, C. (1995). *The Inner World of the Immigrant Child.* Mahwah, NJ: Lawrence Erlbaum.

Minami, M., & McCabe, A. (1995). "Rice Balls and Bear Hunts: Japanese and North American Family Narrative Patterns." *Child Language,* 22 (2) 423-445.

National Center for Children in Poverty. (1996). *One in Four: America's Youngest Poor* (Abridged). New York: Columbia School of Public Health.

U.S. Bureau of the Census. (1990). Report CPHL133.

Vygotsky, L. (1962). *Thought and Language*. Cambridge, MA: MIT Press.

APPLICATION 2

Respecting All Families

Schools that operate on a single cultural model will have difficulty providing meaningful services to all children. Teachers must be aware that universal lessons and activities directed to a "typical" U.S. child minimize learning opportunities because they do not take into account the unique family background and knowledge-in-progress that each child brings to school.

The following activities will help you discern and celebrate family diversity in the classroom. They will also encourage you to gain knowledge of other cultures, as well as a deeper understanding of your own family experiences. Changes in your own and your students' attitudes and behaviors and in your interaction with classroom families will help you evaluate and plan your program.

■ Value the cultural knowledge children bring to school by acknowledging family diversity through discussion, affirmation and celebration. For example:

1 View linguistic and cultural diversity as strengths (e.g., bilingualism is an asset).

2 Use books and other resources that reflect all kinds of families.

3 Display pictures that children draw of their families, or have each child make a page in a class book titled "Our Families."

4 Discuss feelings and experiences children choose to share about what makes their family special.

5 Avoid family-related activities that potentially exclude some children (e.g., holding a Mother's Tea, making Father's Day cards, creating "family trees").

6 Observe a "Someone Special Day" and have children make gifts and invite significant others of their choice to school for breakfast, a play, a concert or other event.

■ Build cultural continuity between home and school to en-courage parent involvement in school activities. For example:

1 Seek ways to communicate with parents in their home language.

2 Encourage and foster home-language learning by explain-ing to families that language skills learned in the home language transfer to the second language.

3 Invite parents to share cultural knowledge such as tradi-tional stories or songs, or to demonstrate job skills or unique talents.

4 Participate in in-service training courses that will assist you in working with culturally diverse children and their families.

5 Provide workshops for parents on meaningful topics based on their interests and needs (e.g., classes on English language, parenting).

6 Identify any adverse social factors (such as poor nutrition, abuse, homelessness, parental depression, violence and drugs) that may affect your classroom families, and bring in experts to advise staff and/or small groups of parents on more effectively meeting the needs of children exposed to these circumstances.

■ Explore your own family background as well as the diversity specific to your classroom community. For example:

1 Examine how your ethnicity, religion, lifestyle and

economic status guide your perceptions, attitudes and behaviors.

2 Invite speakers to your staff meetings to explain the basic tenets of religions practiced in your school community.

3 Use parent conferences and community resources to increase your understanding of the various cultural groups represented in your school.

a wider circle

The preschool teachers at Cabrillo College's Child Development Center in Aptos, California, still talk about the morning several years ago when a group of children tore around the playground whooping and clapping their hands over their mouths, brandishing their make-believe tomahawks. "We're Indians!" shouted the marauders, who were all White.

From one perspective, it was a classic American childhood fantasy. But for the teachers at Cabrillo, it was a call to action.

Cabrillo's vision of childhood centers on a comprehensive anti-bias curriculum. Admission to the program is tailored to reflect, as closely as possible, the racial, cultural, religious and economic diversity of the community. Each baby doll in the house-play area is a different shade from pink to brown. Little boys are encouraged to cook and dance, and the person who visits to explain how telephones work is likely to be a woman or a member of an ethnic minority or someone in a wheelchair.

In short, Cabrillo is a place where diversity and equality aren't just talked about but daily demonstrated. And yet, without warning, a stereotype can swoop in and take the children by storm. A recent reissue of the Disney classic *Peter Pan*, teachers discovered, had spawned the "wild Indians."

Teacher Eric Hoffman remembers intercepting the group and squelching his own impulse to lecture. "That's interesting," he began diplomatically and then proceeded with questions: "What do you do when you act like Indians?" "Did you see Native Americans doing that somewhere?"

"In the video," came the obvious reply. Eric's explanation that the characters in the video weren't real elicited cool 4-year-old logic: "It was a real TV."

Now in his mid-40s, Eric has been teaching preschoolers for more than two decades. This year he has 19 in his room. Small-framed, White, with wire-rimmed glasses and a salt-and-pepper beard, he exudes a quiet, unassuming force that draws children like a magnet.

"I've found that my first task in teaching about another culture," Eric says, "is to make sure the children realize we're talking about people. It's easy to forget that they may not know this. That's especially true when talking about Native Americans in a school with no Native American families."

In another class, for instance, after Eric had brought in an authentic Seminole doll to "talk" about pictures of Seminole houses, one of his students said matter-of-factly, "Indians aren't people. They're monsters."

"Yeah," another child agreed, "blood-thirsty monsters."

Eric knew then that he had skipped some crucial steps. The importance of breaking down complex concepts and images into child-sized pieces is a central premise at Cabrillo and other developmentally-based early childhood centers. Simply "correcting" a stereotype, for example, may eliminate certain words or behaviors from the classroom, but it is unlikely to change what a 4-year-old thinks. Accomplishing the latter requires concerted empathy on the teacher's part, a willingness to enter into the child's thought processes.

When the ethnic stereotype seized his students' imaginations on the playground, Eric enlisted his colleagues' help in analyzing the behavior and undertaking to change it. They asked each other: What other stereotypical images of Native Americans have the children seen? What, if any, exposure have they had to real Native Americans? What do they know about Native Americans in our area? How can we introduce preschoolers to Native American diversity?

Over the next several months, teachers incorporated simple but particular references to Native American cultures when they talked about general topics like nature, food, houses, tools or art. After they helped the original "warriors" investigate traditional hunting practices of Northern California tribes, generic whooping at playtime gave way to careful imitation of local birds. And they discovered real Native American connections in classroom families.

Julie Olsen Edwards, founding director of the Cabrillo Center and currently a professor of education at the college, recalls a moment near the end of the semester: "A couple of kids came in and started doing tomahawk play, and one of the four-year-olds said, 'That's going to hurt Mary's feelings. Her Grandma's an Ohlone.'"

That statement, Olsen Edwards observes, embodies a whole chain of cognitive and emotional connections: First came some concrete information about Native Americans, which the child then linked to the life of her friend. From the friendship arose her recognition of the stereotype's real consequences and, from there, the impulse to respond.

Beyond Diversity

Engaging children's emotions and helping them find the courage to take a stand against bias, says Olsen Edwards, are long-range goals of programs like Cabrillo's. "That's one of the big differences between what I see as an equity program as compared to just a diversity program." But she cautions that considerable groundwork and cultivation are required before the seeds of activism can sprout.

In her classes for prospective teachers, Olsen Edwards identifies four essential steps in early childhood equity education:

1. Helping children develop a sense of pride in and a language to describe their own heritage.
2. Exploring differences of all kinds.
3. Building on children's notions of fairness to create a sense of justice and the capacity to recognize bias.
4. Helping children find ways to confront and eliminate biases they encounter.

For 3-year-olds, Olsen Edwards says, the capacity to describe one's own heritage means being able to say, "In my family, we have Hanukkah" or "In my family, Mama speaks Spanish; Daddy speaks Spanish and English."

Eric Hoffman urges parents into the process. "I want to know more about these cultures. I want each of these families to see its culture reflected in my classroom. But most of the handy 'cultural tips' I've read don't get me very far past stereotypes." He recalls a Costa Rican mother who explained, "Don't expect my son to know that song just because we speak Spanish. We never sing that in my country."

Eric says that his motto in parent relationships is *Take people seriously*. "Whatever comment or criticism or suggestion a person comes up with, I must assume that it carries that person's individual and cultural perspective and deserves my respect.

"For example, a parent might say, 'If she swears at adults, I want you to smack her face.' Then I'd say, 'It sounds like you really want her to learn to respect adults. I agree — that's important for me, too. I don't hit children, so maybe we can figure out something we both can agree on.' And then we talk. I have to take the lead in finding common ground.

"Multiculturalism is such a tricky balance," Eric continues. "My own culture, biases and knowledge must be balanced with the cultures of the families I serve. I can't maintain that balance alone. When I share what I'm trying to do with others and make them a part of the process, I find that people are more willing to tolerate my failures — I'm not expected to be perfect. Perfection is a trap. If you wait until you meet every possible objection, get it all right, you will never get started."

In the second step of the anti-bias curriculum, teachers begin talking with children about differences, a subject that Olsen Edwards believes is innately fascinating for this age group. Physical differences like skin color, hair texture, gender and body type are obvious places to start. Family differences become apparent as children learn more about each other's background and home life. Ranging more widely, by means of books and pictures and stories, a class might investigate the various ways that people around the world eat or sleep or celebrate birthdays.

Olsen Edwards says, "It's what my husband, who's an anthropologist, calls 'anthropology for three-year-olds.' When we don't give them language to talk about difference because *we're* so scared of it, it becomes something that children feel as forbidden and dangerous.

"I was at a parent meeting at another school where they were talking about a kid saying very loudly on the bus, 'That lady's fat! What a fat lady!' and the mother getting really embarrassed and trying to just shush the child up. We talked about what a difference it would have made if she could have talked about different people having different bodies, and not shushed it. What a help it would have been for the woman who got called 'fat,' as well as for the child, to make it a real conversation."

Eric Hoffman also advocates lifting the taboo on talking about difference, but he stresses, "Some comments by children can inadvertently hurt another person. I've been trying to figure out how to support children's inquisitiveness while teaching them about social standards. My main strategy has been to discuss the concept of permission: 'You're very interested in that person's size. We can talk to her about it if we get her permission first, because some people don't mind being talked about and some do. Do you want me to help you ask her for permission?'"

Eric acknowledges that the idea flies in the face of custom — most discussion of people's "differentness" takes place behind their backs. Children, he adds, often say "No!" to the suggestion at first but want to try it later on. "Most adults have been surprised and grateful when asked. They know that everyone just pretends not to notice their differences."

From Image to Action

With the wealth of multicultural posters, books, videos, dolls and other materials available, most early childhood teachers make at least some effort to represent various kinds of diversity in their classroom environment. The Cabrillo program trains teachers to look deeper than the images of race, culture and gender on their shelves and walls. How, Olsen Edwards asks, are the children *using* the environment? Who is playing with whom and with which toys? What books are children choosing?

Gender equity is one of the center's particular concerns: Are the boys favoring one play area, such as the block or truck space, while the girls gravitate to the kitchen or dress-up corner?

"Put them in proximity to each other," Olsen Edwards advises, "so the play can overlap. When we found that boys weren't using the household stuff indoors, we put some of it outdoors in the sandbox. I've done things like have 'girls' hour' at the carpentry table, and suddenly the girls who've never used it show up. I've had 'boys only' dance time. I don't do that long-term, but as a way of starting kids in and getting them to begin to claim something as their own."

Olsen Edwards believes that, as children learn to understand and appreciate diversity rather than fear it, they naturally become attuned to bias. Step three of the Cabrillo curriculum focuses on how a young child's self-centered notions of "fair" and "unfair" enlarge into concepts of justice.

"Some of our four- and five-year-olds can pick up on the word 'stereotype,'" she says, "but most of the time we talk about what's 'true' and what's 'not true.' We talk about how things that aren't true hurt people's feelings and what that's like."

Following a conversation with (or about) the large lady on the bus, she suggests, a parent might say, "You know, some people look at people with big bodies and think 'Just because you're big I'm not going to like you.' And some people look at somebody who's little and think 'Just because you're little I'm not going to like you.' Isn't that awful?"

Olsen Edwards emphasizes, "A three-year-old can pick up the injustice of that, but it's got to be made specific and articulate. It's hard, because we're sort of falling over our own tongues. Language is an approximation, and it's far more approximate for children than it is for grownups. I think one of the big mistakes of adults is to think that if a child can say something, they understand it. Conversely, that if a child can't say it, they don't understand it. The match between what they've experienced and the words they are capable of using is not great.

"The place where there's the greatest overlap is in highly tangible 'object' stuff, where kids will agree that that's a block and that's a ball. And if they're given an opportunity to develop a language for feelings, they can match words and feelings pretty well. But when you get into abstract concepts, you've got to go in tiny little increments, and you've got to be prepared to do it again and again, from a lot of different directions."

Center director Nancy Brown explains, "We don't use the vocabulary of 'share,' 'fairness' and so on. We don't say, 'You must take turns.' We want them to *construct* an understanding of what it means to share. We'd say, 'It looks like you both want to go first,' and then help them figure out why that's impossible."

When children themselves use a word like "share," says Eric Hoffman, "then it becomes our job to say, 'Oh, you want to share. Let's talk more about that. What does that mean for you?' Because there are so many different ways to do it. For some children it might mean 'I use it first and then you get to use it' or 'I get to decide what happens, and you can be the little baby.'"

Eric is careful not to reduce sharing to the equal distribution of materials. "My focus is never on the toys. It's 'Can I help these children form a relationship?'"

While Cabrillo teachers avoid using shorthand terms for the intricacies of getting along, they find that often the best remedy for antisocial behavior is to call it as they see it. "We had a situation last year," Eric explains, "where there were a group of boys who were going into the bathroom [a shared alcove off the classroom] and poking at girls' bodies, making fun of their bodies. 'Harass' was a very appropriate word for what was going on. I defined it for them and said, 'I will not allow you to do it.'

"I said to the girls, 'If someone is harassing you like that, you can say: "Don't harass me!"' It was really effective. [The behavior] stopped within a few days."

"Threaten" is another big word that Eric finds useful. "It comes up over and over again: 'If you don't give me the ball, you can't come to my birthday party.' Everybody says those things, but to have them labeled a 'threat' makes the kids see it as a bigger deal. I can say, 'I won't let you solve this by threatening him.' 'Tease' is too soft a word."

Perhaps no word carries more of a stigma at Cabrillo than "exclude." Olsen Edwards says there is one basic rule: "You can't exclude anybody because of who they are. Ever. To say, 'You can't play here because you're a girl, because you're a boy, because of your skin color' — that's who a person is, and you can't exclude them on that basis."

She is quick to add that there *are* legitimate reasons for refusing to play with someone. Undesirable behavior is one. "You can say, 'You can't play here because you pushed me down' or 'You can't play here because you tore up the dolls' or 'You can't play here because when you yell it hurts my ears.' Kids make the distinction. We say it often enough with enough examples, and they begin to get it."

When exclusion by category does occur, says Nancy Brown, the teacher's task is to challenge the child's narrow view of who *can* be included. One useful technique is what Brown calls "sportscasting." When a conflict arises, the teacher asks simple questions in order to construct a "play-by-play" narrative and elicit ideas for solutions.

In the kitchen area, for instance, a girl might tell a boy that boys can't play with the dishes. On the abstract level of the stereotype, Eric Hoffman avoids simply refuting it, as in, "That's not true. Boys *can* play with the dishes." Rather, he looks for the hidden logic: "You haven't seen many boys play with the dishes. I wonder why that's true. At my house, I'm the one who usually sets the table and washes the dishes." Later he might invite a male chef in to create a salad.

But on the concrete level, the play problem is still there. To "break down" the immediate conflict, Eric asks each child what he or she would like to do with the dishes. The girl might say, "I want to have a party for my friend," and the boy might say, "It's dinner time, and I have to wash the dishes."

"As an adult," Eric says, "you can see that those two ideas could really mesh, but the children can't see that. I can come in and say, 'Oh, *you* want to play a party game, and *you* want to play a dish-washing game. How are we going to solve this problem?' Very often they will come up with a creative solution: 'Oh, I'll wash the dishes for your party,' and all of a sudden the two games get connected, and the children get connected. Everybody has to say 'Yes' to an idea before we can say the problem is solved."

Sometimes, Olsen Edwards points out, what may look like exclusion by category really has more to do with mastering group-play skills than with rejecting differences. "You have to know your children and pay attention to them and their age and what's going on. If you've got three little girls who are dancing with scarves, and a boy comes up and they exclude him because he's a boy, then I deal with them on it.

"But if the reason he's being excluded is because they're trying to figure out how to play as a threesome, which is a really hard number, I'm going to support them in doing that. But it becomes my job to find a way for him to be dancing with scarves. It may mean that the next day I need to sit down and ask myself: 'How are we going to do some dance stuff around the Center that's going to include more boys, so he's not the only one?' It's the adult's responsibility to create the environment that makes that happen."

In Olsen Edwards' view, the multicultural movement has made significant progress in equipping young children to talk about difference and even to recognize bias. But the trickier matter of *eliminating* bias has too often been left up to adults. In the same way that we teach children to "stand up for themselves," she says, Step 4 in the Cabrillo sequence helps them do the same for each other.

"When we had a child here a few years ago who was wheel-chair-bound most of the time, it became everybody's responsibility to make sure Breanna could get to where we were going. The kids helped invent little ramps. When they built a bus out of blocks, it became the job to figure out how to get Breanna on the bus. She was a part of our community. We all had a responsibility to find a way to make it work for her."

The little girl who halted the tomahawk play, says Olsen Edwards, was acting on the same principle. "The early childhood world has done a lot of glorifying of autonomy. I think autonomy without deep community is a disaster."

Cabrillo teachers see preschool as the ideal place for fostering such interdependence. Because social development is already a central focus for this age group, every incident of stereotyping or exclusion gives the teacher an opportunity to reinforce classroom relationships — by supporting any child who is slighted or left out, by encouraging anyone who speaks up about it, and by helping the offender hear how others feel.

"Their day is full of little injustices," says Eric. "I want to help them develop skills and discernments that will enable them to address larger injustices later in their lives. I want them to know that injustice is not overcome by magic or wishes. People make it happen. *You* can make it happen."

Enlarging the Classroom Community

While teaching in several California preschools in the early 1980s, Eric Hoffman attracted the attention of the Cabrillo College education faculty for his commitment to equity issues and his effectiveness with both children and parents. He accepted an offer to teach a few adult courses and acquired some "remedial" training of his own in the bargain. In 1986, he was hired to his current position as a master teacher in the college's laboratory nursery school.

Eric knew that his every move would now be scrutinized by student teachers and other observers from behind the big two-way mirror in his classroom. But his sense of purpose and his hard-won insights gave him the confidence he needed. Then he met the "Pink Connection."

The other teachers had already coined the name for a clique of 4-year-old girls who, Eric says, "spent much of their day disrupting the classroom by trading clothes, arguing about who would wear whose pink and lavender outfit, and ostracizing anyone who failed to meet their fashion standards." In the first few weeks of school, they had successfully intimidated the entire class. Every morning, they commandeered Circle Time by turning their backs to the teacher and noisily swapping socks.

Eric realized he was going to have to stage his own "counter-coup." In desperation, he borrowed two flannel cut-out figures from a colleague and began playing out the girls' disruptive behavior on the story board. As "Betty" and "Saul" scrambled around dressing and re-dressing and playing fashion police, everyone started to pay attention. The commotion on the board became more interesting than the tiresome antics of the girls.

That night, Eric cut out a whole pink and purple wardrobe, and he spent the rest of the week focusing the circle on clothes. With each variation, the children got more involved: "That's Betty's favorite jacket." "Don't put socks on their ears!" "Saul can't wear pink boots!"

Having regained control of the circle — and thwarted the "Pink Connection" — Eric planned to retire the cut-outs and return to his usual sing-along and storybook routine. But Saul and Betty were taking on lives of their own. Every day, the children had new questions: How old are they? Are they brother and sister? Do they live with their mom and dad? Do they ride the bus to school? When Eric tossed the questions back for group discussion, he found surprising consensus on most details — everyone seemed to want the evolving story to move along. Suddenly, the classroom community had two new members.

For Halloween, the children determined that Betty would dress up as a bird and Saul as a squirrel. In the spirit of the holiday, Eric decided to add a bit of mischief. He told the class that Betty wanted a big mask. But Saul was afraid of masks and didn't even want her to wear one.

"Then I asked the same question I often used when helping with disputes in the classroom: 'How can we solve this problem?' I had struck gold! The conversation that followed was thoughtful and serious." Prompted by questions from the teacher, the children discussed their own feelings about masks and scary costumes. "The group came up with ideas, debated choices and selected one: Saul would wear a hat and Betty a mask, but when Saul felt scared, Betty would take off her mask to show that she was still Betty."

The success of the Halloween problem-solving encouraged Eric to tackle more complicated issues using the flannel figures. After lengthy discussion, for example, the class debunked a gender stereotype by deciding that Saul should be able to wear the pink boots if he wanted to.

Eric admits that he "didn't start this process with equity issues in mind. I was just trying to survive as a teacher. But by using the same problem-solving language and routines throughout the day to discuss everything from science questions to social disputes to puppet problems, I later realized that I had created a comfortable framework for investigating diversity."

One October Tuesday, Eric rhythmically strums his Autoharp as the children of Cabrillo preschool begin settling into a circle. He sings softly, "Everybody, come sit at the Welcome Ta-a-a-ble." Around his neck hang multicolored pieces of macaroni on a string. An easel prominently displays a dog puppet and two flan-nel cut-out children. A whole assortment of cloth characters are integral members of Eric's class. Marisol and Juan, for example, are Mexican American siblings.

This morning, Harvey — a puppet Eric frequently uses "to break the rules" — asks Juan to play hide-and-seek. At first, Har-vey and the children hide from Juan. Then Harvey proposes hid-ing Juan's Snoopy dog and other toys. Everyone, including Juan, is having a good time until Harvey suggests hiding Juan's glasses.

For several weeks, the class has been exploring the sense of sight, including the various things people use to help them see better. They have inspected the classroom and each other using binoculars and magnifying glasses and mirrors.

"Action, that's what does it!" Eric says. "I always ask myself, 'How can I support my Circle Time discussion with a related activity that preschoolers will dive into, a setup that is hands-on, interesting and fun?'"

Though none of the children wears eyeglasses, they have learned what Eric's do and that he has to take care not to lose or break them.

"No!" shouts 4-year-old Michael as Harvey the puppet reaches toward Juan's face. "That's not fair! He couldn't see!"

Eric later reflects on the moment: "Sometimes you get that far and sometimes you don't. That's my goal: to get them to see that a situation isn't fair to someone different from them. It will carry on with them when they're older. I see it as sowing seeds." ★

REFLECTION 3

Fairness

"Fair" and "no fair" are two of the first moral judgments that children learn to make. For most young children the criteria are simple: Fair is whatever suits me; no fair is whatever does not. The egocentrism behind these subjective standards accounts for one of the biggest challenges preschoolers face — the difficulty of learning to take turns and share.

Young children use the concept of fairness both to comply with and to resist adult-imposed rules. One study of preschool and kindergarten classrooms found that children who were strongly discouraged by teachers from using violent strategies such as hitting, shouting, pushing and snatching instead adapted existing classroom rules to assert privilege and power (Jordan, Cowan & Roberts, 1995).

To illustrate: Raj is at the computer, and Jessica wants to use it. She claims that it is her turn and reminds Raj that he had his turn yesterday. By invoking the rule of "sharing and turn-taking" to define what is "fair," Jessica tries to gain immediate use of the computer. Raj does not relinquish his position. He uses the rule of original possession, or "I was here first," to conceptualize "fairness" from his perspective. From an assortment of class rules, children select the one they perceive as benefitting themselves in a given situation.

As children's social perspectives broaden at ages 4 and 5, a more egalitarian notion of fairness emerges: The teacher supposed to treat everyone the same. This idea affirms t moral dimension of the teacher's role. It is through their c capacities of honesty, courage and fairness that teachers

engage children in active communication about rig\
responsibilities (Sockett, 1994). Respecting the entitleme\
others becomes a basic building-block of community.

A purely objective, quantitative fairness, however, is inco\
plete. In the first place, it reduces an essentially moral capac\
to a matter of bookkeeping — the equal distribution of good\
and privileges. Further, it assigns the responsibility for fairness\
to a single "dispenser," the teacher. And, perhaps most impor-\
tantly, it creates the illusion that being fair is easy.

Fairness in the early childhood classroom has many dimensions. On the teacher's part, one goal of fairness is to give all of
the children an equal sense of security and well-being. A set of
consistent rules and specified consequences for their violation
provide both a model for each child's own behavior and an
assurance of protection from the misbehavior of others. Rules
that promote sharing and turn-taking ensure that all children
have access to resources, spaces and equipment.

Beyond the framework of explicit rules, fairness becomes
more complicated. Integral to a child's sense of security and
well-being is feeling appreciated as an individual. "Equal treat-
ment" can sometimes ignore the unequal needs and strengths
children bring to the group. On a given day, one child may need
to sit in the rocking chair because her mom is sick, and someone else who uses crutches might need an extra turn at kickball. When students understand that the teacher's response to
these differences is a sign of caring for everyone rather than
favoring a few, their notion of what is fair enlarges. The young
4- and 5-year-olds' "equal shares" solution changes as they
understand the necessary balance between group and individual considerations based on need and merit (Edwards, 1986).

By modeling a flexible and sensitive fairness in all relationships, the teacher encourages children to treat each other fairly

and introduces them to one of the basic responsibilities of citizenship. As the child's frame of reference widens, the experience of fairness in the classroom becomes a vision of justice in community and society. *(See also* Classroom Rules and Discipline, *p. 158.)*

References

Edwards, C. P. (1986). *Promoting Social and Moral Development in Young Children.* New York: Teachers College Press.

Jordan, E., Cowan, A., & Roberts, J. (1995). "Knowing the Rules: Discursive Strategies in Young Children's Power Struggles." *Early Childhood Research Quarterly, 10,* 339-358.

Sockett, H. (1994). *The Moral Base for Teacher Professionalism.* New York: Teachers College Press.

A P P L I C A T I O N   3

Nurturing Justice

The transition from the toddler's egocentric worldview to the preschooler's understanding of the needs and wishes of others is a formidable — and formative — event in early childhood. The equitable classroom provides continual opportunities for children to both practice and benefit from fairness. The "skills of fairness" develop through play, as well as observation of peer and adult interaction. Dialogue with caring adults is another important influence.

The activities presented below assume that a major goal of early childhood education is to foster children's ability to balance their own needs and wishes with those of other individuals and the group as a whole. Careful attention to children's questions and concerns about fairness will help teachers refine the selected activities.

■ Encourage dialogue to identify social issues important to children. For example:

1 Create settings that are conducive to talking and listening (e.g., a circle for groups and quiet private areas for one-on-one discussions).

2 Establish simple and clear protocols for turn-taking during discussions.

3 Encourage whole-group dialogue among children rather than relying on teacher-child question and response.

4 Summarize, comment on and suggest alternatives for children's remarks and thank them for their contribution.

- Design learning activities that help children explore the concepts of fairness and justice. For example:
  1 Use dramatic play, interviews, and puppets and other props to talk about social and moral dilemmas.
  2 Read selected children's literature to discuss or act out hypothetical social and moral problems.

- To expand the sense of fairness into a vision of justice, begin carefully involving children in school and community social action. For example:
  1 "Adopt" a group such as a nursing home or a homeless shelter and have children make something or perform a service for the group on a biweekly or monthly basis (e.g., create art decorations, perform songs or skits, collect food and blankets).
  2 Invite to your classroom community helpers whose job is to provide social services, then follow up with activities about social-service occupations (e.g., skits, art projects, activity centers).
  3 Do something meaningful for the school that addresses a social problem, and discuss how the action promotes fairness (e.g., inspect your building for accessibility to the physically challenged, pick up litter or create a bulletin board for the main office that addresses a social/moral issue).

Gender Awareness

Even before they can say the words, most toddlers become adept at pointing out girls and boys, women and men. Gender appears to be one of the first dimensions of identity that young children perceive in self and others. An understanding of the developmental processes young children undergo to acquire information and form attitudes about gender can help early childhood teachers foster gender equity in the classroom.

Children draw their earliest conclusions about gender from obvious traits such as clothing, hairstyle, body shape and the pitch of the voice. A little later, they begin to learn about the body parts that make boys and girls different. This fascinating subject leads to serious — and sometimes startling — questions as cognitive and verbal skills develop. The time-honored game of "Doctor" and other behaviors also reflect the power of gender curiosity in early childhood.

Between the ages of 4 and 7, children come to realize that being male and being female are permanent biological conditions. In turn, they comprehend that changing one's clothing, interests or activities does not change one's gender.

Around this time, children start to expand their ideas about gender to include not just what people *are* but what they *do*. This broader sorting is first expressed nonverbally through play. Experts disagree as to the relative importance of "nature" and "nurture" in influencing boys' and girls' playing styles and activity preferences. Most parents and teachers, however, find that children are remarkably receptive to such cues, whatever their source.

According to psychologist Phyllis Katz (1987), children acquire the social "content" of gender awareness in three sequential stages. First, young children learn the culturally appropriate behavior for boys and girls: the toy, activity and playmate choices expected of each gender. In this stage, they establish firm boundaries around gender roles, often self-segregating by gender in their play groups. It doesn't take them long to assert these patterns verbally: "Girls can't throw"; "Boys don't play with dolls."

Next, children learn the expectations associated with adult male and female roles. As they attempt to interpret the adult world, many children make broad assumptions and generalizations: "Men can't cook"; "Mommies don't drive tractors."

In the third stage, children act out adult gender roles based on these concepts. For example, during pretend play, girls become mothers, nurses and teachers, while boys are the fathers, firefighters and doctors.

The information children use in constructing gender knowledge comes from a variety of sources — families, peers, media, teachers, children's books and instructional materials. A significant portion of what they learn about gender occurs informally. Parents influence emerging gender concepts directly and indirectly through the toys they purchase, the roles they model in the home and the ways they respond to gender issues in children's behavior.

Research shows that family characteristics such as structure, socioeconomic level, class, culture, race and religion can significantly shape children's "gender learning." For example, Katz (1987) reports that young Latinas, as a group, showed a higher degree of gender stereotyping in their occupational aspirations than did White and Black girls. In the same study, girls who came from single-parent families, regardless of race or ethnicity, showed the least amount of gender stereotyping.

Researchers have confirmed Kohlberg's (1966) theory that gender stereotyping among both boys and girls ages 5 to 7 often entails a preference for the "male" role because it is more exciting and powerful (McCormick, 1994). Cultural affirmation of this preference is evident in the differences in status accorded by labels such as "tomboy" and "sissy" or "Daddy's girl" and "Mama's boy." In addition, gender stereotyping can distort children's perception of non-stereotypical role models. When 5- to 7-year-olds were shown pictures of adults in nontraditional roles, such as a female physician and a male nurse, most reported that they had seen the reverse (Signorella, 1987).

Such evidence suggests that gender stereotyping in children's own thinking can have an adverse effect on the social and cognitive development of both girls and boys. Teachers who model gender equity in the classroom and intervene appropriately to counteract gender bias recognize these actions as essential steps in celebrating the self-worth, abilities and potential of all children.

References

Katz, P. A. (1987). "Variations in Family Constellations: Effects on Gender Schemata." New Directions for Child Development, 38, 39-56.

Kohlberg, L. (1966). "A Cognitive-Developmental Analysis of Children's Sex-role Concepts and Attitudes." In E. E. Maccoby (Ed.), The Development of Sex Differences (pp. 82-173). Stanford: Stanford University Press.

McCormick, T. M. (1994). Creating the Nonsexist Classroom: A Multicultural Approach. New York: Teachers College Press.

Signorella, M. L. (1987). "Gender Schemata: Individual Differences and Context Effects." New Directions for Child Development, 38, 23-38.

A P P L I C A T I O N   4

Fostering Gender Equity

As young children develop gender awareness, they establish rigid lines around gender roles. This gender sorting is expressed in work and play through preferences in toys, playmates and activities. To foster gender-role flexibility in their students, teachers can organize classroom environments and conduct lessons that encourage boys and girls to engage in cross-gender cooperative activities.

The following guidelines can help teachers incorporate a nonsexist model that rewards the abilities of both girls and boys. Explore and evaluate how these activities can help children expand their perception of gender boundaries.

■ Create a classroom environment that encourages interaction between boys and girls in all aspects of work and play. For example:

1 Integrate seating arrangements and mix genders when assigning group work.

2 Create learning areas with nonsexist materials that encourage full participation of both girls and boys.

3 Forbid derision based on gender, and encourage inclusion in all activities.

■ Examine curricular resources to eliminate gender bias. For example:

1 Identify and eliminate language that denies female participation (e.g., replace "fireman" with "firefighter"; avoid use of "he" as a generic pronoun).

2 Inspect books, posters and bulletin boards for gender balance and varied gender characteristics and roles.

3 Aim for gender balance in the characters, both real and imaginary, that you discuss in class (e.g., celebrate male and female heroes).

■ Consider how the "hidden curriculum" encourages gender stereotypes and take steps to counteract the process. For example:

1 Evaluate any differences in behavior expectations and discipline practices toward boys and girls.

2 Observe how you handle emotional issues with girls and boys (e.g., do you attempt to distract crying boys but reassure crying girls?).

3 Examine your use of praise (e.g., make sure that compliments for working quietly and neatly or being brave and strong apply equally to both genders).

4 Practice gender equity in the assignment of classroom duties (e.g., help boys and girls take equal responsibility for moving tables, cleaning up after snack and dusting shelves).

5 Break down gender stereotypes through your own actions (e.g., a female teacher fixing a wagon or a male teacher mending a doll's dress gives children a broader sense of their own capacities).

6 Provide opportunities for children to engage in activities that challenge gender stereotypes (e.g., as a mixed gender group, design and build a simple bookcase, or make chef hats and have everyone cook a feast).

7 Arrange for adults to visit the classroom to model nontraditional roles (e.g., invite female carpenters and male nurses to talk about what they do).

from the ground up

A t Elmwood Primary School in Shawnee, Ohio, there's a big colorful replica of a locomotive in the main hallway. You can't look far in this sprawling modern facility without seeing a railroad crossing sign — a bright yellow circle quartered by a black "X," with an "R" on either side. In the carpeted corridors, in the "open" classrooms, on coffee mugs and pencils, and on badges and stickers that teachers and students wear proudly, the emblem is everywhere. One obvious assumption might be that these people are obsessed with trains.

But the signs tell another story. A couple of years ago, Brenda Ellis, a speech pathologist who spends most of each week at Elmwood, attended a workshop on learning disabilities. There she heard someone speak about the need to teach respect and responsibility to special education students.

"I thought, 'Hey, that's not a bad idea for all kids,'" Ellis recalls.

Back at school, she shared her thoughts with colleagues and helped to assemble a steering team to explore the possibilities.

The team identified particular social goals that teachers wanted to help their children achieve: to respect themselves and others, to accept and appreciate diversity, to take responsibility for their actions, to tolerate opposing viewpoints, and to contribute to the school community. A common refrain became the team's unofficial motto: Kids can't practice what they haven't been taught.

"We can't expect that it's already been done at home," says Amber Potter, who assumed principalship of Elmwood in 1994 after 10 years as a primary teacher. "We can't expect that all of them know how to be here in this little society and how to interact appropriately."

Teachers realized that, with 600 students under the age of 8 — most of whom can't read — the message would have to be rendered visually. As the staff brainstormed for a symbol to drive home the theme, custodian Bob Wallace offered a suggestion: "It came to me that we have to respect railroad crossings," recalls Wallace. "Why not use a railroad crossing sign? The two 'R's could stand for Respect and Responsibility."

Everyone loved the idea. Most rules of behavior, teachers realized, embodied one "R" or the other, or both. Parents were commissioned to paint the symbol onto signs that now festoon the entire facility. "R & R" badges and stickers became handy reminders to practice respectful, responsible behavior, such as using polite language, taking care of materials and considering other people's feelings.

The insignia has special resonance in this suburb of Lima (pronounced LIE-ma), which originated as a railroad hub. "Most of the children probably see the R & R sign at least twice a day out in the community," Ellis explains, "coming to and from school. It's a constant reminder. And," she adds with a smile, "we hope they remember it's also a railroad sign!"

For Ellis and her colleagues, the orderly Elmwood atmosphere is proof that, with hard work and clear goals, even the most ingrained patterns of interaction can be transformed.

On a recent morning, a typical 2nd-grade conflict flared up in an instant. Brendan and Darren had just stepped back proudly to view the bookshelves they had straightened in teacher Rosemary Mullen's room, when Mark, oblivious to their efforts, pulled a book out. A dozen neighboring volumes toppled over.

To 7-year-old eyes, the damage must have appeared deliberate and irreparable. Summoning the outer limits of their vocabulary, Brendan and Darren lashed out at Mark in righteous rage, and he collapsed into hard sobs on the floor.

"I started to intervene," recalls Mullen, "but they were so shocked that he was crying that I waited to see what would happen."

The two boys walked over to their distraught classmate, sat down next to him and apologized. "I'm sorry, Mark," one said. "We thought you were messing up our books." As the other circled an arm around him, Mark's tears subsided.

New Connections

Until 1993, the Shawnee school district had two K-5 schools: Elmwood and Maplewood, just a few miles from each other but worlds apart. The landscape along the flat two-lane roads crisscrossing Allen County reveals the contrast, as the modest homes and trailer parks sprinkled in Elmwood's neighborhoods give way to the spacious, manicured subdivisions and designer homes near Maplewood.

"The perception was a rich school/poor school thing," says district superintendent Bill Lodermeier, a familiar face around Elmwood. "Maplewood was viewed as the academic elite. Elmwood was known as just 'The Fort.'" The nickname clearly carried derogatory overtones; it referred to Fort Shawnee, an older municipality within Shawnee's boundaries where many of Elmwood's poorer children lived.

The hardest lessons concerning Elmwood's stigma fell on students moving into 6th grade, when the two school populations would merge at the middle school. "All the graduating fifth graders of both schools would play soccer in the summer," says Lodermeier. "And then when they went to sixth grade in the fall, the kids from Maplewood would stick with their old school groups, and the Elmwood kids were excluded. It was subtle, but it was real — a sense that 'We're friends in the summer, but we can't be friends now.'"

Lodermeier proposed a solution: Create a single primary school for grades K through 2 at Elmwood and turn Maplewood into a school for grades 3 and 4. The matter could have been decided at the school board level, but Lodermeier opened it up to the parents for their input. Many parents, particularly those whose children were already attending Maplewood, would have preferred to leave things as they were. Parents on the planning committee, however, were more concerned about the overcrowding that was already taking place at Maplewood. Continuing the status quo would have meant renovating and expanding the school. The new arrangement went into effect at the end of the 1992-93 school year, after Lodermeier personally interviewed all 50 teachers involved before he determined staffing for the two schools.

For the teachers, Potter recalls, "It was a hard summer spent moving, but the kids never missed a beat. They were fine from day one."

Whereas the previous school setup had reinforced an existing division in the community, the restructuring forged a new bond. "The kids are on common ground now," says Lodermeier.

"They're getting the same education. They're in Girl Scouts, Boy Scouts together. They play soccer together in the summer, and now they stay together as friends in the fall. It's a unifying approach."

Economic differences aside, Elmwood has by most measures a relatively homogeneous school population. Altogether, the African American, Asian American, Latino and Native American children enrolled constitute 12 percent of the student body; the rest are White. Brenda Ellis is the only African American staff member. Fewer than 10 percent of the children have learning disabilities, physical disabilities or other special needs. Yet, appreciation for diversity is an explicit Elmwood theme.

"Back when I was a student, my world ended in Ohio," says Lodermeier, who is White. "Today a kid's world is global. That's hard for a lot of parents to understand. We have to teach tolerance, because the opposite is completely out of the question. Intolerance in society today is not acceptable; our world — the economy and society — won't survive it."

Educators and others who visit Elmwood — an IBM software test site — to observe students interacting with computers are frequently surprised to see how well the children interact with *one another.* As visitors quickly learn, the atmosphere is no accident: At Elmwood, social skills are explained, drilled and reinforced the same way reading and math skills are.

The fundamentals of sharing, making friends, cooperating and resolving disagreements, says support teacher Rosemary Mullen, are just as essential for future success in school and life as the academic basics. This concerted approach to positive behavior reflects an ongoing process — from the district office on down — of rethinking the role of public schools.

Bill Lodermeier's personal goal is to create a school where children feel part of a community and teachers feel free to innovate, take risks and develop creatively. A risk-taker by nature, Lodermeier easily sheds his administrative and political persona to sit on the floor next to a shy child or to gallop unannounced into a classroom with glitter on his hands, claiming to have nearly caught a leprechaun down the hall.

At the beginning of each school year, he shows teachers a video tape that illustrates respect for diversity: In a song performed by Harry Chapin on the "Tonight Show," a little boy asks a teacher what color to make some flowers. "Red," the teacher says, in a tone of voice that suggests there is no other color. When the child gets to the next grade, a teacher asks him why all his flowers are red. "Because," he answers firmly, "that's what color flowers are."

There are no pat answers at Elmwood. "I want teachers to take chances," says Amber Potter. "The failure is in not trying things. People who want to do the same thing every year frighten me."

Ground Rules

The organic approach — seeking improvement from within and involving everyone in the process — sets a high standard for staff commitment and creativity.

"We're still evolving," Potter observes, "but I want this school to be a true primary center where every child feels successful. I want it to be an active place to learn.

"And when the kids leave Elmwood, I want them to be not only academically ready, but also socially and emotionally ready — confident in themselves and their abilities, and confident in making good decisions so they don't have to rely on their peers. I want them to know that it's OK to be different, and that everybody doesn't have to agree."

One recent afternoon, counselor Bonnie Siferd read the familiar story of Peter Rabbit to a 2nd grade class. She asked the children what was likable about Peter, and she got many answers — his fuzzy ears, his funny tricks and the way he always ends up in trouble with his mother or Mr. McGregor. Then Siferd read the story again, this time asking the children to look at Peter's pranks from Mr. McGregor's point of view: What is it like to tend a garden when someone is always sneaking in to steal your cabbages?

"We want the kids to see that there's always more than one side to a story," says Siferd, "so before you can begin any kind of mediation, you have to see opposing viewpoints. At this age, the kids are so egocentric they have no idea that there's any other point of view. So here, we point out that while Peter Rabbit is cute and fuzzy, he's also a thief."

Each month, often in partnership with the Lion and Lamb Peace Center at nearby Bluffton (Mennonite) College, Siferd works with teachers at Elmwood to develop classroom presentations on a specific topic relating to tolerance or conflict resolution. Follow-up activities encourage children to talk about hypothetical problems and to raise real issues of their own.

For one session, 1st and 2nd graders created a "Differences Train": Each child cut out a paper railroad car and drew on it a self-portrait. Linked with pins and arrayed around the classroom walls, the train became a visual reminder of both individuality and cooperation. Out in the hallway, the children decorated a giant toy train — formerly a department-store display prop — with pictures representing different cultures.

The next day, teachers led class discussions about the many forms of diversity. Some brought in apples — Red Delicious, Golden Delicious, Granny Smith. "How are they alike and how are they different?" the teachers asked. "Is one better than the other?" "Does anyone have favorites?" Other teachers brought teddy bears of all shapes and sizes for the children to compare.

Children are capable of discerning physical differences like skin color and hair texture from an early age. However, Brenda Ellis finds that, in the students' eyes, her role as caregiver often blurs the fact that she belongs to a different race than most of them. In her workshops for 1st graders, for example, when she points out that she is a member of a group called Black or African American, White students frequently respond, "No, you're not."

In one exercise on "same and different," several White children sorted themselves with Ellis in a comparison of skin colors. While identification across racial lines is a basic goal of programs like Elmwood's, Ellis stresses the importance of respecting differences rather than denying them.

"I explained to the White children, 'We're the same in many ways, but in this way, we're different.'" Later, when she asked the students to compare hands, many of the White children realized for the first time that their hands, too, were of varying shades.

Categories don't set children apart at Elmwood. Students with multiple handicaps are mainstreamed as much as individual abilities permit. Lila, a child with Down syndrome, for example, is in a regular classroom for all but 40 minutes of the day.

Before Lila arrived, her mom came to talk to the 1st grade class her daughter would be joining. She showed family photographs and told the children about Lila's birth. After explaining the effects of Down syndrome in simple terms, she talked about the ways in which Lila and her classmates were alike.

When Lila came to school, the children enfolded her with love and attention. They were so inclusive, Bonnie Siferd notes, "that, if anything, they shielded her from the kind of open discussion they might have liked to have had." Similarly, Helen, who has cerebral palsy, always has plenty of help pushing her wheelchair, and no one protests when Barry, an autistic child who does everything in twos, demands a second turn. One child, called down for teasing a special-needs classmate, protested, "But I was teasing everybody else, and I didn't want her to feel left out."

Each of the 30-plus students with special needs has an individualized education plan that emphasizes inclusion. When a child needs special assistance, the facilitator works with him or her in the regular classroom. Siferd does most of her counselling in the classroom setting, and Mullen does academic intervention there, as well.

"We have so many kids and teachers coming and going to so many different places," says Amber Potter, "that getting special help is not the stigma it once was."

This year, some fissures opened in the tolerance theme — not around racial or developmental differences, but around friendship and cliques. As with most children this age, it was not uncommon to hear a student say to another, "I'll like you only if you don't like her" or "If you're going to let her play, I don't want to play with you." The problem, teachers noticed, was worse among girls.

A focal point of one clique's activity was the cafeteria. Every day, this select group decided who would eat with whom the next day, and if they would buy lunch or bring their own. Not to receive this inside knowledge was considered equivalent to banishment; if a child came to school thinking that her friends were going to bring packed lunches and discovered that they had instead decided to buy, she was left out. The staff first learned about the exclusionary behavior when a mother called to say her daughter had a stomachache because she dreaded going to school.

"I might expect this kind of behavior among fifth and sixth graders," Rosemary Mullen observes. "I was shocked to find it in second graders."

Mullen and Siferd decided to try to shed some light on the cliques and build a sense of community among the girls. During one play period, Mullen and the classroom teacher sent the boys out to recess and put the girls in a circle in the activity room. Siferd did the same with another class.

The teachers asked the girls to write down a list of things that were bothering them and read them aloud to the group. One by one the tiny, hurt voices chimed in. "Mandy said you wouldn't be my friend if I played with somebody else at recess." "You want to be my friend one day and then the next day you don't." And Mullen told the group that she had overheard one of them saying, "I don't like you because you like so-and-so."

While the culprit squirmed, Mullen asked the group to think about the remark. "How would it make you feel to be told that?" she asked them. "How would it make the girl who was named feel? Why should someone like one person only? Do you know how many friends I have?"

The questions led to a discussion of "how sometimes we say things that hurt people's feelings — sometimes we mean to do it, and sometimes we don't," Mullen says. "But we need to know that the ground rules at school are that we do our very best to get along with everybody, that we can think whatever we want to think, but we may not *say* whatever we think.

"There was a lot of defensiveness at first, a lot of 'But she's' and 'But I's,' but we kept bringing it back to the issue: How would *you* feel?"

She asked the girls to start noting any hurtful things that happened to them so the issues could be identified and discussed at group time. After that, the group met twice a week for a month, sometimes in the circle and sometimes out on the playground. A pair of former adversaries recently wrote to Mullen, "We're getting along much better now."

The "girls only" meetings were a bit out of the ordinary, Mullen acknowledges. But they helped focus the girls' attention on the feelings they all had in common. "We got calls from parents who were amazed at the change."

Peers for Peace

Every day at lunchtime, Elmwood hallways are dotted with purple T-shirts, the badge of honor for 2nd graders who, by completing their work and behaving well, have earned the privilege of being "peacemakers." Recommended by their classroom teachers and trained by counselor Bonnie Siferd, the peacemakers help their peers and younger schoolmates — and sometimes their elders — put the Elmwood ideals of Respect and Responsibility into practice.

Bill Lodermeier recalls hearing an assertive 2nd grade voice behind him one morning saying, "You're walking very well today. How do you spell 'Lodermeier'?" When he turned, he saw a purple-shirted peacemaker filling out a good behavior ticket. "'Mr. Bill' will do," the superintendent said.

Positive reinforcement is the peacemakers' tool of choice. Students who follow hallway and lunchroom rules about walking safely, talking quietly and keeping tables and floors clean receive citations that accumulate into bigger rewards.

In concert with the peacemaker patrols, Elmwood's staff lavishes praise and attention on students who are "caught being good." Examples of helpfulness and kindness are reported in loudspeaker announcements. Snapshots of commendable individuals and groups appear on hall bulletin boards.

"You don't learn self-esteem," says Rosemary Mullen. "You only get it through success. And if they do what we teach today, they're successful."

Brenda Ellis believes that the program has turned peer pressure into an asset. "Before," she remembers, "Bonnie Siferd and I had hall duty, and it was a chore. Then the peacemakers came, and I asked Bonnie, 'Why are we here?' The children were so effective."

In the classroom, rewards and reprimands take the form of easily understood symbols for performance. A bulletin board in each kindergarten room displays a paper "pocket" for every child. When someone breaks a rule, the teacher places a yellow, or warning, Popsicle stick in his or her pocket. A second infraction the same day warrants replacing the yellow stick with a red one and taking five minutes off the child's recess.

In one 1st grade room, the rules themselves are color-coded, with sticks to match: The red rule is "Be kind"; the white rule is "Follow directions"; and the blue rule is "Look, listen, think and participate." Teachers say the visual system helps children identify their own behavioral strengths and weaknesses. An empty pocket at the end of the day merits a ticket, redeemable on Fridays for trinkets or snacks. Cooperative 2nd graders earn "behavior bucks" that they can "spend" for rewards such as bubblegum, stickers or small toys.

Rosemary Mullen emphasizes that blind obedience is not the goal. "Last week, a child came up to me and said, 'If this is a free world, why do we have rules?' I thought it was a very good question. I asked him to tell me a rule that he didn't understand, and he said, 'Running. I don't know why we can't run.' I said, 'You can run — outside,' and he said, 'But not in school.' So we acted out what would happen in certain situations if you ran instead of walked. And then it made sense."

Students come to Mullen's room for structured play — a time to vent a little energy and practice skills for getting along. Each session begins with a "praise-phrase circle," in which students take turns telling others what they like about them or asking questions to get to know them better. Each day two new children are picked to receive the attention.

"You're nice," someone says to Martine on one occasion. "You're funny," says another. Then two in quick succession: "I like you because you always listen to me" and "You help me when I need it." A classmate asks Raymond, "Do you have any pets?" and the long list that follows includes two lizards. When Mullen's turn comes, she says, "I like you, Raymond, because I remember when you came to us new last year, and it was a pretty brave thing to get to know a lot of children and be nice."

Being nice, teachers attest, is the glue that holds Elmwood together. But when niceness wears thin and conflict happens, a clear set of guidelines helps restore the community bond. Over and over, the children hear the steps for resolving conflicts repeated, along with encouragement to practice them: What is the problem? What are the possible solutions? Are they good choices or bad choices? What's the best one to try? Then let's go do it!

"It's a broken record," Siferd laughs, "but it's a proactive philosophy. We believe that if you give kids the skills, they'll be able to cope with new situations that they meet. We tell them, 'You do have power because you make choices.' They learn that 'I and only I am responsible for my thoughts, my feelings and my actions.'"

Principal Amber Potter observes, "It's not always apparent to children what the problem is. Two different children perceive the problem to be two different things. Sometimes just because it's a problem for somebody else doesn't mean it's a problem for me. So to get them to agree on what the problem is takes a lot of work."

When an argument, a shoving match or a name-calling session breaks out in the hallway or the lunchroom, the nearest purple-shirted 2nd grader rushes to the scene. If the combatants don't agree to the help, an adult is summoned immediately. But if they agree to arbitration by the peacemaker, they must listen to each other, brainstorm for options, agree on a tentative solution and try it out.

A few procedural rules — no name-calling, no interrupting, and always telling the truth — help the process run smoothly. Although not every student earns the right to be a peacemaker during the year, all 2nd graders get the training. The program has been so popular that last year's "graduates" asked to continue it at their new school.

Near the principal's office is a Peace Wall, each paper "brick" of which represents a conflict that has been resolved. The wall grows as children add drawings to illustrate their mastery of the peace process.

"Little children," says Amber Potter, "often can't see on their own that there is another choice besides the one they made. Our problem-solving shows them that, if a choice they make puts them into an uncomfortable position or an undesirable situation, there are other choices. Democracy is about learning to make wise choices within your freedom."

Elmwood teachers recognize the larger societal implications of the R & R program, but their immediate hope is small-scale — that the children will remember to be nice from one moment to the next. "We're worried about whether what we teach them in the classroom will transfer to the hallway, the playground, the cafeteria and the bus," says Bonnie Siferd.

Rosemary Mullen adds, "We practice being nice in all these different settings and hope that eventually it will come together."

The "Uh-Oh" Feeling

Sometimes the most effective behavior modification is accomplished by the students themselves. One boy repeatedly interrupted the class by yelling back at the teacher, refusing to do things and disrupting others. One day, when he was absent, the teacher asked the class if they had any suggestions for solving the problem. "He's always saying everybody hates him," they noted. "Maybe we could smile, say 'good morning' and include him in the group."

Now and then, a more direct approach is necessary, Bonnie Siferd says. "There are some kids who just don't get it, and it takes a confrontation by peers who say, 'We're really tired of the way you're acting, and if you really want to be with us, you have to clean up your act.' It's very closely monitored, and it's not done in a cruel way, but we say, 'Tell him why you don't want him to play with you.' Many times, one instance like that equals the teacher intervening over and over."

Every student needs to practice appropriate behavior in order to be accepted, Siferd says. "If you're knocking down the other kids' blocks or you're totally belligerent or rude, you are making choices that could lead to being excluded. If you're willing to share, that's a good choice. But if you're stingy or bossy or not able to take turns in terms of materials and attention, then you may not be included. We're encouraging the minimum social skills that would allow a child to fit in anywhere as a contributing member of the group."

Over and over, Elmwood students learn that their own personal choices have an impact on their school society. One year the 2nd graders produced a video illustrating proper behavior in the playroom, the hallway, the lunchroom, the playground and the bus. Now the same video is shown to the lower grades every September.

Although learning appropriate behavior can be harder for some children than learning math or reading, every student shows some progress. One day at the end of the school year, Lila, who has Down syndrome, decided to test the limits in the playroom: She knocked one student's blocks down, took Lincoln Logs away from another, and removed the clothespin that held a classmate's drawing, letting it fall to the floor.

Mullen made her sit in a chair for a few minutes before asking her if she could play right and not repeat any of those behaviors. Success, Mullen explains, is sometimes weighed in small increments:

"At the beginning of the year she would have power-played me — big. She would not have gone over to the chair, she would have tugged at my hand, she would have yelled and screamed. But she took her medicine and went back to play. In the last year, she's learned to play with other people, to help build something instead of going off on her own."

In contrast to the child who understands generalized rules such as "Kind words, kind hands" or "Three strikes, you're out," Lila receives more specific instructions and reprimands tailored to her cognitive development. While her classmates sometimes find Lila's behavior frustrating, seeing teachers apply appropriate expectations — and consequences — helps them to respect developmental differences. The same process gives Lila a way to fit in.

"There is a consequence for bad behavior for everyone, including the differently abled child," says Mullen. "It wouldn't be fair to let her get away with it, because then we would be teaching her that being different allows her to be a bully."

Mullen measures larger triumphs by the reduction of her own active role. "By February or March, I have to do much less intervening," she says. "They just work things out on their own. If there are too many people to play a certain game, they'll say, 'Well, when I get tired, I'll let you know and you can take my place.' And then you'll hear someone saying, 'I'm done now. Come over and you can have a turn.'"

Having the confidence that they can solve problems enables the children to be more successful in uncharted waters. Recently, one class wanted to make their own rules for kickball: the girls against the boys, with no outs. An inning consisted of each team's entire lineup. They played happily for the entire period, and there was no arguing or fighting. The teacher stayed in the background only to make sure that everyone was safe.

Setbacks do occur, occasionally shaking the staff's confidence in the program. One morning near the end of the school year, a girl inked the new jacket of a neighbor and then denied that she had done it. A boy who thought a classmate had deliberately pulled a chair out from under him slapped her.

Discouragement is only temporary, however. "They only learn respect and responsibility by doing it and doing it and by hearing it and hearing it," Bonnie Siferd says. "I don't want to give us an excuse to say they're too developmentally young and their inclination is to be impulsive rather than thoughtful and considerate. I don't want us to explain away why it can't work just because it's difficult. As a fellow staffer said, it's difficult to teach reading, but we certainly don't give up on that.

"Our goal for the children, whether they are able to be tolerant on a consistent basis or not, is that they would at least have the 'uh-oh' feeling — the voice of conscience — so that even if they haven't made very good choices, they will know they haven't. And, hopefully, the 'uh-oh' feeling will not be very comfortable, so that the next time they'll do it better."

For 2nd graders, mastering the skills of respect and responsibility can seem like a long journey. At Elmwood, there are plenty of markers to keep them on the right track. ★

R E F L E C T I O N   5

Friendship Connections

To have a friend and to be a friend are more than wishful expectations in early childhood — they are basic needs. Considerable evidence suggests that friendship supports young children's cognitive as well as emotional development. Children who relate to others in socially acceptable ways are usually well-liked and included in play and work activities. Factors that hinder or disrupt the emerging bonds of friendship can have lasting negative effects on children's lives.

For most young children, school is the primary place to develop a sense of social belonging, to form ideas about friendship, and to practice the skills necessary for making and keeping friends. A teacher's affection and respect toward all children provides not only a nurturing environment but also an important model of friendship.

Children's need for peer connection develops sequentially. Infants as young as six months crawl toward and "check" other babies for information or signals that might involve them in a social interchange. Toddlers often display a preference for certain partners in "parallel play." Intermittently, they may interact with each other and even create imitation games: One child picks up a block, and a few seconds later a peer copies her; or one says "Da" and another mimics the sound.

The word "friend" enters many children's vocabulary in the early months of speech, reinforced by frequent adult references. Pets, playmates and toy creatures may all receive the label. A 2-year-old may point to someone who shares his table or plays with him at school and exclaim, "That's my friend!" The designation reflects the pleasure and comfort of emerging social routines (Edwards, 1986).

For 3- and 4-year-olds, friendship takes on a more intentional aspect. Preschoolers and kindergartners confer and withdraw the status of "friend" at will according to a number of criteria, including general compatibility, variable moods and the nature of the present activity. At this stage, comments such as "Will you be my friend?" "You're not my friend!" or even "I hate you!" are not literal expressions of emotion but rather perceptions of the momentary prospects for play. Although children may experience disappointment and even anger at a rebuff during playtime, such feelings generally reverse at the next positive encounter.

Around ages 6 through 8, children's friendships acquire a more sophisticated and lasting content: Friends are people who are nice to each other; they exchange resources and services; and they maintain a relationship over time. Children at this stage begin to share secrets, toys and promises with their friends. They may also choose to terminate friendships if they perceive that a partner refuses to help or ignores their feelings or needs. These feelings and experiences provide the groundwork for the mutual respect and responsibility that characterize mature friendships.

At all developmental levels, children exhibit varying degrees of success at making and keeping friends. The skills required for positive social interaction come naturally to some children and prove more challenging for others. When a class member has difficulty establishing friendships, it is important for the teacher to understand the situation at hand as well as other possible sources for the problem. There is a distinction between children who lack friends because they lack social skills and those who are targets of bias, prejudice and discrimination by their peers.

In the case of the former, guided activities can help the individual child master sharing, control aggressive tendencies or meet other challenges. When a child is excluded because of a difference in language, race, appearance, gender, ability level or other factors, it is the teacher's responsibility to intervene with both reassurance to the victim and corrective instruction to the peers involved (Derman-Sparks, 1995). Children who consistently isolate themselves or who display excessive aggression may require referral to a specialist.

Healthy peer relationships empower children to develop social competence, embrace egalitarian attitudes and handle conflict effectively. Early childhood programs that incorporate friendship as a major curricular component prepare children for a respectful, responsible role in their expanding world.

References

Derman-Sparks, L. (1995). "Children and Diversity." *Early Childhood Today,* 10 (3) 42-45.

Edwards, C. P. (1986). *Promoting Social and Moral Development in Young Children.* New York: Teachers College Press.

APPLICATION 5

Building Friendship Skills

Teachers can play a significant role in helping children develop the ablility to initiate and sustain friendships. As their conception of friendship changes over time, children can build on basic social skills to make lasting connections.

The following suggestions are designed to promote positive relationships in the classroom. One of the simplest ways to assess children's social competence is to observe their interactions with others. The degree to which a child is liked or disliked can also serve as a barometer of social adjustment. Changes or lack of change in children's behavior will assist you in planning and modifying intervention strategies.

■ Celebrate the importance of friendship in developmentally appropriate ways. For example:

1 Read books, listen to music and view videos with friendship themes.

2 Have children draw pictures of themselves playing with friends, and label and display the artwork.

3 Make a list of what friends do or what friendship means.

4 Discuss how it feels when a playmate moves away, and create going-away friendship books for children who are moving.

5 Prepare and present skits and role-plays in which friends are an emotional resource (e.g., offering hugs, sharing materials, having fun together).

■ Intervene when discriminatory or exclusionary behavior is

harmful, and provide positive models for forging friendships. For example:

1 Set limits to gender segregation and provide opportunities for cross-gender friendships.

2 Use puppets, stuffed animals, skits and interviews to model inclusive behavior and appropriate actions children might take to stand up for themselves.

3 Purchase toys, books and materials that encourage sharing, empathy and cooperation.

■ Build on the concept of friendship to create community. For example:

1 Plan joyful whole-group activities such as singing, dancing and marching, and hold performances for other classes or invited guests.

2 Provide opportunities for noncompetitive games that include everyone.

3 Make badges, T-shirts, posters or banners that include each child as a member of the classroom community.

4 During play, work, snack times and festive occasions, call attention to the good feelings of belonging and acceptance.

5 Emphasize cooperation and commitment by having children work toward long-term common goals (e.g., plant a garden, keep a memory book chronicling the class's shared history).

R E F L E C T I O N   6

Sameness

The lesson that "we are all alike, and we are all different" is a fundamental premise of many early childhood programs. Often, teachers reason that children can learn to appreciate the outward differences among classmates from diverse groups by discovering their hidden similarities. Sometimes, however, the process must occur in reverse. In classrooms where all or most children share a significant outward trait such as race, the path to appreciating diversity begins with the discovery of hidden differences.

For many young children, cultural pluralism exists somewhere far away from home, neighborhood or classroom. They may encounter racial, ethnic and economic diversity in the larger community and in the media, but the people they know directly are, by these measures, "the same." While the difficulty of adequately addressing racial, ethnic, cultural or class differences in the school setting is widely acknowledged, perceived sameness in these dimensions presents its own special challenges for teachers.

The problem is evident in the selective use of two terms to describe schools or classrooms that lack obvious diversity — *homogeneous* and *segregated*. The phrase "homogeneous school" suggests a range of images, from privilege, comfort and familiarity on the one hand to blandness, rigidity and parochialism on the other. Frequently, however, the description carries a pointed implication — all-White and middle class. By contrast, "segregated" conjures a more static vision, one associated with negative factors such as poverty, discrimination and marginality.

American Indian reservation schools, Asian schools located in international districts, Black inner-city schools and Latino barrio schools are commonly described as "segregated."

Integration Inequities

The actions of school policy-makers often reflect this lingering historical dichotomy. For example, many school districts across the United States use exemplary magnet programs featuring enhanced resources and special teacher preparation to attract White families to formerly "segregated" schools. These programs, often created in response to federal mandates, are presented to White parents and teachers as advantageous to their children's academic, social and economic future.

The corresponding movement of racial-ethnic minority children into previously all-White schools, by contrast, is unlikely to focus on "selling points" tailored to the incoming families' needs or preferences. Racial-ethnic minority children are expected to adapt to and benefit from the existing White school culture. No special programs or resources await them or their teachers (Hollins, 1996).

In spite of federal law and local initiatives promoting school integration, student populations in many districts continue to reflect residential segregation by race, ethnicity and class. Making children comfortable in a pluralistic world remains a formidable task, especially in settings that lack obvious diversity. Young children need to interact in relationships that are spontaneous and meaningful in order to acquire a working knowledge of racial, ethnic and cultural distinctions.

Research shows that sporadic and incidental contact provides only rudimentary tools for discerning surface differences (Helms, 1990). Thus, while multicultural resources are useful in monoracial classrooms, they are not sufficient. It cannot be assumed that anti-bias posters and books, ethnic foods, minority guests and cultural celebrations in and of themselves promote in young children a deep understanding of cultural diversity.

Diversity in Monocultural Classrooms

No curriculum can remedy the effects of racial isolation. However, teachers *can* help children explore dimensions of pluralism and discover that all people originate from diverse and complex backgrounds. In classrooms of racially similar children, diversity comes in myriad forms — beliefs, learning styles, personalities, family incomes, family structures, intellectual-creative-social-physical abilities, and on and on. Differences in all these attributes offer opportunities for enriching children's sense of individuality and equity.

While teachers can begin by using basic lessons — grouping those wearing or not wearing red, those who walk to school and those who come by bus — to build a conceptual understanding of sameness and difference, they can expand this knowledge by introducing activities that acknowledge diversity in more meaningful configurations. Often the best curricular lessons are those that use the resources at hand.

The diverse ethnic heritages of White children, for example, offer rich possibilities that often remain unexplored. However, research indicates that White children must learn more than their ancestors' countries of origin if they are to develop an ethnic identity (Alba, 1990). For example, children who identify as "Irish" or as being "from Germany" can deepen these self-concepts by exploring the values and cultural contributions of these ethnic heritages.

Although some racial-ethnic minority children also attend "homogeneous" schools (e.g., all-Black, all-Hawaiian or reservation schools), these children are often taught by White teachers, are usually exposed to positive images of White people in books and the media, and generally have at least some personal interaction with Whites — for example, in businesses or community services. Accordingly, the task for teachers in homogeneous minority schools is not to "introduce" diversity but to promote equity and positive identity development. Exploration of hidden differences can serve both of these goals.

Children in any classroom have no difficulty discovering cultural diversity among themselves. They often refer openly to home celebrations, religious observances and family lifestyles. Teachers can encourage such sharing and incorporate the resulting discoveries into daily social-academic school life.

In the preschool and early primary years, children learn to internalize positive attitudes about differences and transfer them to new situations. As they learn to respect self and value others, they can, in time, expand the idea of "others" to include a wider range of racial, ethnic, cultural and economic dimensions.

References

Alba, R. D. (1990). *Ethnic Identity: The Transformation of White America*. New Haven: Yale University Press.

Helms, J. E. (Ed.). (1990). *Black and White Racial Identity: Theory, Research, and Practice*. New York: Greenwood Press.

Hollins, E. R. (1996). *Culture in School Learning: Revealing the Deep Meaning*. Mahwah, NJ: Lawrence Erlbaum.

A P P L I C A T I O N   6

Discovering Diversity

Diversity in all forms plays a role in shaping the social environment of classrooms. Teachers in all-White classrooms are often concerned that their children might develop beliefs, attitudes and values that reflect a narrow range of differences. Likewise, teachers with classrooms full of racial-minority students must be aware of the pervasive, negative messages in schools and society that may encourage these children to feel inferior to Whites. Teachers in any setting can prepare students for a pluralistic society by helping them discern and value the multiple dimensions of diversity.

To evaluate the following suggested activities, reflect on changes in your own and your students' perceptions of "same" and "different." Appreciation for diversity at hand can be used to cultivate a commitment to equity and justice in the wider society.

■ Examine how you and your students treat others who are perceived as different/threatening or those who make you uncomfortable. For example:

1 How do you and your class make "new" students feel welcome?

2 How do you address the problem when classmates exclude particular children?

3 Do you handle diversity issues such as gender equity differently from other diversity issues, such as children's cruelty to a student who is differently abled physically or intellectually, or the exclusion of homosexual parents from parent-teacher committees?

4 What actions do you and your students take when you see racially motivated injustices against particular children present in the classroom or statements made about people from other racial-ethnic groups?

■ Help children appreciate the diversity within their own racial, ethnic or cultural group and family. For example:
  1 Discuss differences and similarities in children's home traditions and rituals (e.g., birthday celebrations, meal and bedtime routines, or relationships with relatives and significant others). Encourage children to find other characteristics to compare and contrast.
  2 Group children heterogeneously in organized play and work activities (e.g., by gender, popularity, religious orientation, ability and economic status) to provide the broadest cross-section of sociocultural interactions.

■ Instill in children the knowledge that differences in physical traits, cultural backgrounds, abilities and perceived needs and preferences are valued in the classroom. For example:
  1 Involve all children in decision-making about classroom activities and rules so they can see each other and their actions as critical components of their world.
  2 Reinforce the concept that differences contribute to the richness of the classroom community (e.g., differing opinions help us think about the same idea in new ways; creative problem-solving gives us more options to choose from; the ways different children find to illustrate the same story give us more pictures to enjoy).

a sense of wonder

At the start of each day, Linda Alston sits in a child's chair, her eyes at child's-eye level, as her 25 kindergartners line up to shake her hand.

"It's a bonding ritual," Linda says. "They love it. They look forward to it. God forbid I should be late getting here and my assistant has had to get them started. They will each still come up to me to shake their hand, so that says to me how important it is for them."

Frequently, the morning handshake even draws older students back to Linda's room. Sixth graders, she says, will sneak out of their classroom and join in on their knees so they can be short again. "I don't even see them until the end of the line comes up, and here they are behind my little kids!"

The formal daily greeting is not just for the children's benefit, admits Linda, an African American mother of three. "It's very important to me, too, just looking into their eyes. That's the time in the day that I can count on to connect with each one simply person-to-person — not teacher-to-student or even adult-to-child."

Little formalities are a big part of life in Room 7 at Denver's Mitchell Elementary, a public Montessori school on the city's northeast side. After 4-year-old Susanna graciously invites her classmate Carla to join her for a snack, Linda prompts Carla to respond in kind: "Thank you, Susanna. I accept." (Just as important, Linda later points out, is being able to say, "No, thank you. I decline.")

When a guest speaker visits, a designated "host" presents a bouquet of cut flowers "on behalf of Room 7." At some time during the year, each child sends someone special a written invitation to come for tea. A small, lace-covered table in one corner holds a shiny silver teapot, china cups and crisp linen napkins.

"Grace and courtesy" stand alongside language, mathematics and other more scholarly disciplines in the Montessori curriculum. Linda points out that the acquisition of simple social graces is a developmentally appropriate goal for kindergartners. Teaching children to be polite, she believes, teaches them respect for themselves and others.

"If we start out by learning to say 'thank you' to someone who gives us something, to say 'excuse me' if we bump someone or to say 'please' if we want something, it's a consciousness-raising activity on an elementary scale. It's making us conscious that 'This is a person, and I want to treat this person the same way I would wish someone to treat me.'"

On the way to the map table, Teddy bumps Paulo and Paulo gives Teddy a shove. The little disturbance ripples. "Class," Linda calls calmly from across the room, "what kind of children are you?"

"Peaceful, loving children!" answers nearly everyone, including the two edgy boys. For kindergartners, reciting a collective response to a simple question is often an effective way to "regroup."

"Thank you," says Linda. "Now show me what that means."

Teddy and Paulo eye each other warily, then shake hands. Harmony, these youngsters are learning, takes practice.

Toni Robinson, whose 4-year-old daughter, Amani, is in Linda's room for the second year, views common courtesy as a foundation for later attitudes and responsibilities. "If you see that at this young age," she says, "imagine how as adults they will look at the world and deal with the world and make choices in the world in a different way."

Mitchell Elementary is located just north of Denver's Five Points intersection, formerly the heart of the city's African American community. At one time, thriving Black-owned businesses lined the surrounding blocks. Today, the neighborhood is predominantly Mexican American, and on the commercial streets a few stores and restaurants survive among mostly abandoned buildings.

In 1983, when a federal court ordered Denver to bring its school system into compliance with existing desegregation requirements, Mitchell was picked as the pilot school and won a federal grant to fund its conversion to a Montessori program. Principal Martha Urioste arranged free Montessori training for her faculty, but no one accepted the offer. As a result, she began to recruit teachers locally, regionally and nationally.

"Once word got out," Urioste recalls, "people began calling from across the country." Paula and Paul Biwer, both Montessori teachers from Milwaukee, were hired to coordinate the conversion. They persuaded their former colleague Linda Alston to move west.

The new program was phased in one level at a time over seven years, beginning with kindergarten. As the planners had hoped, the Montessori magnet drew an unprecedented diversity of families to Mitchell School. Linda Alston's class this year includes

African American, Asian American, Latino, Native American and White children; one boy was born in Uganda and another in Thailand. Some live in two-income households, while others have single parents who are unemployed. The only drawback to the magnet program, in Linda's view, is the nature of its "magnetism." Because Mitchell Montessori was designed to attract White families to an inner city school, it serves only a small percentage of children from the predominantly non-White immediate neighborhood. The rest are bused to a school some distance away.

To many teachers and parents, "public Montessori" sounds like a contradiction in terms. The educational philosophy introduced by Italian physician Maria Montessori in 1907 is practiced today mainly in private academies around the world. In recent years, however, the program has drawn the attention of U.S. public school systems seeking creative means of desegregation. Administrators find that Montessori magnet schools, now numbering more than 100 nationwide, can help maintain a racially as well as economically diverse population within the public schools.

Linda Alston acknowledges that the Montessori method, with its requisite training and classroom materials, is prohibitively expensive for many public school systems to adopt. But she encourages parents and teachers to adapt ideas freely from Montessori or any program that works.

"There are wonderful things from Montessori that you will find being practiced in many traditional classrooms across the country," she says.

A Well-Loved Place

Linda's concept of grace and courtesy extends beyond verbal politeness to a respect for each child's physical space and the whole classroom environment. The children use small rugs to define their individual work areas, and by mutual agreement any project-in-progress left unattended on a rug will remain undisturbed.

Linda spends the last three weeks of summer vacation "rigging" her room with world art she has collected, potted plants and child-sized home furnishings. The result is a kind of multi-cultural coziness: A Navajo spirit-catcher hangs near the window. Kente cloth forms a bulletin board backdrop. A reading nook beside the aquarium features a mini easy chair, a table lamp and books about all kinds of children. High over the whole space stretches a banner proclaiming "We Are One."

The most striking element of the decor, however, is the rainbow of real flowers that brighten not just Room 7 but all of Mitchell School. Linda had long considered fresh flowers for special occasions one of her necessary out-of-pocket expenses for the school year. When she came to Mitchell eight years ago and began to patronize a neighborhood floral wholesaler, he offered her a discount on flowers that had been in the warehouse for more than two days. These "distressed flowers," he explained, were perfectly good blossoms with a full week's life left in them, but his retailers wouldn't accept them.

One day on her way out, Linda noticed a dumpster brimming with beautiful daisies, carnations and asters just like the ones she had paid for. "What's wrong with this picture?" she asked herself. With some friendly persuasion, the owner agreed to let her have the throwaways for free, and a classroom parent volunteered to make a weekly pickup at the warehouse.

Linda finds that working with flowers offers her students benefits at many levels — beautifying their environment, improving their manipulative skills and developing their aesthetic capacities.

"Flowers are so soothing for children," she says. "The most wound-up child can work with flower arranging — see the brilliant colors, smell the fragrances, feel the water — to create something beautiful. It's very affirming and peaceful for them."

The vagaries of flower arranging can sometimes lead to unexpected discoveries about beauty itself and the magic of the artistic process. Recently, as 4-year-old Edwin was beginning an arrangement, a zinnia accidentally slipped down into the glass vase half full of water. Linda recalls that "suddenly here was this wonderful abstract image of a beautiful flower, magnified inside the vase, which I'm sure Edwin never intended to happen. He cut the stem too short, and the zinnia fell in. But he looked at it and thought — just as any artist would — 'Hey, I like that!' So it sat there, and it was so beautiful I invited his mother in to see this one-of-a-kind creation."

In Linda's view, every child is an artist, just as each is a storyteller and a musician, a dancer and a teacher. She respects their contributions no differently than she does the more official capacities of adults. On the Room 7 Logistics Team, every child gets to try out half a dozen "professions" that rotate by the day. Amani the Historian announces, "Today is Thursday, May 17th," as she changes the number on the calendar. Jack the Meteorologist observes, "It's raining outside and the sun isn't shining."

"Is it going to rain all day?" the teacher asks. Jack nods.

Juliet, today's Zoologist, feeds the resident lizards, guinea pig and fish, while Corey the Botanist waters the plants. In addition to helping the classroom function as a community, Linda believes, rotating professions teaches children the ABC's of career choice and equal opportunity. The simple tasks required for each role are early lessons in how the world works, who does what, and why each job is important.

At this age, Linda says, "they're so full of inquiry and enthusiasm and infinite possibility. They live their whole lives out of the context of 'Why?'" Respecting each child's natural sense of wonder helps Alston remain open to the unexpected.

As she sees it, innocent curiosity gives young children a decided advantage over adults in bridging differences. "There's no inhibition," Linda says, "about 'Should I say this?' or 'Should I ask that?' They want to know why somebody else is a different color, or why her hair is curly and somebody else's hair is straight, and why he looks this way or they dress that way. So they just ask.

"That's how they get along, because they're not afraid to ask anything they want to know. They learn more about each other that way." The "grace and courtesy" curriculum, Linda notes, sensitizes children to the importance of expressing their curiosity respectfully.

An important task for the teacher at this level is to help children avoid the snares of stereotyping and of assigning relative values to external traits. Jerry Brown, a friend of Linda's who is a university professor and a member of the Kutenai/Salish tribe, visited Room 7 last spring to talk about his Native American heritage and teach the class a song in Lakota, the language of his father. When he demonstrated a few verses and asked for questions, Amani said, "Your voice sounds funny."

Brown replied that maybe that was because she didn't know the Lakota language. Once she learned what the words meant, he suggested, they might not sound so strange. The answer satisfied Amani, but later, after Brown had finished his presentation, Alston returned to the point. At the Ellipse, a large oval on the carpet where the class has group time, she reminded everyone of Amani's remark.

"If you were going to visit another school, or another country, how would you feel if somebody said, 'Ooh, that girl talks funny!' or 'Ooh, that boy sounds funny!' How would that make you feel?"

"Sad," said Patrice.

"Upset," offered Sami, whose English carries the accent of his native Uganda.

"I know I would feel that way," Linda agreed. "That's why we do all these things we do in our classroom. So that when you hear something different from the way you talk or you see a different way that someone dresses or a different food that someone eats or a different way they sing or tell a story, then we can learn about it instead of saying it's funny. Is it really funny, like when you laugh at something?"

"No!" the class chimed.

"If it's not funny, maybe we can find another word to describe something we're not used to hearing or seeing or tasting. Who can give me an example?"

"Different," someone said.

"Nice."

"New!" said Teddy.

Linda praised these suggestions and led the class in an exercise of complimenting one another and then reporting how they felt in response. The consequences of words — positive and negative — are a recurrent theme in Room 7.

"I always like to bring it back to an affective kind of experience," Linda says. "To say, 'Boys and girls, we shouldn't say something sounds funny, because that's not nice' is just not enough. That's just the *should.* But when I ask 'How would you feel if ...?' — then we have that moment where they can really reflect and notice in their bodies how they are actually feeling."

The inner experience of empathy, Linda believes, is the lifeblood of multiculturalism. "It's not enough just to say, 'Here are some facts about Native Americans or about African Americans.' We have to create something that comes from the heart, to find our commonalities."

When Linda returned recently from a trip to China, her students added several Chinese words and phrases to their international vocabulary. (They could already greet one another and count to 10 in Spanish, Swahili and Thai.) Fluency, of course, is not the goal. Rather, Linda hopes to instill in them a sense that the vast array of world languages serve a single purpose.

"As soon as a person starts to experience something and own it for herself," she says, "then she feels 'It's mine now, so certainly I'm not going to think that there's anything bad or inferior about it.' If they know words from other languages, then when they hear that language spoken it's an 'Aha!' moment for them: 'Oh, I know *ni hao.* I can say "hello" in Chinese.' I think it even transcends that to include languages they've not heard before. They can say, 'I don't understand it and it sounds very different to me, but I can trust that it is, in fact, a language and a way that other people effectively communicate.'"

Expanding the Rainbow

Children's perceptions of and responses to difference, Linda realizes, often extend beyond the reach of easy lessons. She listens and watches for signs of confusion or fear. One such instance centered on the colors of the small work-rugs in the classroom. The gray ones are sturdily woven of good-quality yarn, but Linda's budget forced her to include several less durable ones, which are white. One fall a new student — a 3-year-old African American boy — asked, "Do the Black children use the dark rugs and the White children use the white rugs?"

Linda heard in this question a plain truth about the world. "Sad to say, at that early age he was getting the message that somehow Black people get certain things or can use certain things and White people get to use certain things. I told him, 'You can choose whatever color rug you want to use.' He was fine with that, but this is why it's necessary for me not to keep my head up in the clouds and pretend, 'Oh, I don't see color and nobody sees color, and we're just all in the world together.' That's why I consciously teach tolerance."

The language we use to talk about race, she says, is part of the problem. "Black" and "White" are only conventional racial labels, not accurate descriptions of skin color. These polarized terms bring a whole set of connotations to racial identity. Negative popular images of the color black, Linda and other educators believe, can have a harmful effect on the self-images of African American children — and on the perception of African Americans by children of other races. Yet many teachers never use black in their classroom decoration except for Halloween witches' robes and bad-luck cats. Whether they grasp particular meanings or not, children hear the negative messages of terms like *black eye, blackmail* and *black hole,* in contrast with the positive associations of *white knight, white collar* and *snow white.*

To address the problem, Linda has developed a unit on black-and-white art. She brings in examples of black-and-white decorative work including drawings and paintings from many cultures, and the children create their own black-and-white designs from posterboard, construction paper, tempera and markers to adorn the room. In the process, they learn that these contrasting colors are equally expressive and especially vibrant when used side by side.

For one activity, Linda reads aloud Robert Frost's poem "Stopping by Woods on a Snowy Evening" and then has the children illustrate the scene on blue paper using only black and white paint.

"You can bet your last dime," she says, "that when I show them the black paint someone will say it's 'yucky.' That's my opening to ask them 'Why?' Many of them — especially the 'Black' children — have learned to feel negatively toward that color, but they can't offer a good, logical reason. As we probe further, the children begin to question those associations. And as they work on the art, with their own hands they're creating evidence to the contrary — a picture that is black and white and beautiful."

Outward differences such as skin color and language and tradition are just a portion of the diversity that Linda explores and celebrates with her class. One of the most widely varied of all human traits is personal opinion, and she believes it's never too early to acquaint children with the arts of negotiation and compromise.

When Amani turned 4 this year, she and her parents selected four photographs — one for each year of her life — to be displayed as "Amani's Time Line," in keeping with the class custom. The first snapshot showed a tiny baby, still wet from birth, lying across her mom's chest. Everyone thought the picture was great except for one girl, who found it disturbing that the mom's bare hip was exposed. She asked the teacher to take the picture down.

Linda's response was to assemble the class on the Ellipse to discuss the dilemma. Some people look at the picture and see a mother and child, she explained; some people see "no clothes." Then she asked what the group could do to respect these two views.

As Amani's mom, Toni Robinson, remembers, it didn't take long to strike a balance: Someone suggested covering the bare hip with a square of construction paper, so that anyone who wanted to see the whole picture could just lift the flap!

"That's the kind of thing that goes on here," says Robinson. "'We are one.' If a concern comes up with one of the children, they feel that they have a right to express themselves. The solution doesn't have to be 'either/or.' We can find the medium."

Given the capricious nature of young minds, Linda warns, incorporating deliberation and consensus into the early childhood classroom is a risky proposition. But risk, she believes, is an essential ingredient of good teaching.

"Nobody talks about the *intuitive* part of this," she says. "It's even difficult for me now, because how do you explain it? It's like being in love."

She is quick to declare that neither following one's instincts nor "following the child," as Maria Montessori advised, can supply all the answers. "I use many eclectic resources. I'm constantly looking for books. But the person who wrote that book is not in the moment with the child and me. I trust my own expertise there, because I have the context.

"What works for me is to really be in tune and to be a keen observer of the children, and to trust that first thought that comes to me and makes no sense at the moment — I may have no idea why I'm thinking it. But I've learned to trust that consistently now. When I do, magic happens."

First You Need a Village

At her spot on the Ellipse one morning, Linda arranges several framed photographs, a vase of flowers and a boom-box. She asks the children to listen carefully to the tape she's selected — Bette Midler's performance of "The Wind Beneath My Wings." The refrain swells to fill the room: "Did you ever know that you're my hero?"

"Boys and girls," Linda asks as the song ends, "what is a hero?"

Michelle waves eagerly. "Somebody that saves people!"

"Spiderman!" shouts Paulo.

Sami says, "The President."

"When we say 'hero,'" Linda proposes, "what does the 'he' part bring to mind?"

"It's like boys," says Daphne.

The teacher picks up one of the photographs and shows it around. "That's why I like to say 'heroes and sheroes.' Maria Montessori, one of my 'sheroes,' was a brave woman who believed in herself and believed she could be a doctor even though people told her she couldn't because she was a girl."

Most of the children recognize the two men in the next photo — Martin Luther King Jr. and Malcolm X. When Linda identifies the African American woman in the third picture as Mary McLeod Bethune, Patrice announces, "She started a school with 50 cents and a dollar!"

The fourth picture, Linda explains, shows one of her most special "sheroes," but someone the class has probably never heard of. "This is my Aunt Gerry," she says. "Did you know a hero or a shero could be someone in your own family?"

Michelle raises her hand again to offer her own idea of heroic behavior. "My daddy protects me from ghosts because he locks the doors."

Since her own childhood, Linda has felt the influence of local heroes. But it took her a long time to realize that not all children have such beacons in their lives. Several years ago she heard someone quote a young boy's reply to the question "Who would be disappointed if you joined a gang?"

"Nobody," said the boy.

"Now I don't believe that," Linda says. "But what I reflected on later was that it's not important whether I believe it — if that's his perception, that's his reality." The disconnection from family and community that the boy's statement implies crystallized some of Linda's own perceptions of social problems. She began to look seriously at the kinds of role models our society provides its youngest members.

"How many people can be Michael Jordan?" she asks. "Probably just Michael Jordan. Children are constantly being bombarded with 'You're good, you've made it, when you have a lot of money and material things.' That's the message that the gangs present very clearly. They look at people like me, for example, who are teaching school — they can make in one week the money that I make in a whole year." Kids 5 and 6 years old, she says, can stand on the corner as lookouts for a drug house and make hundreds of dollars a day.

Linda reasons that if children are being exposed to such extreme examples at this young age, it's the responsibility of parents and teachers to provide explicit alternatives. "It's funny to me when people say, 'Should we teach values or shouldn't we?' And they get into long debates about it. I always think, 'How can you *not* teach values?' Even if we tried, how could we avoid sharing our values with children?"

The "grace and courtesy" theme, she points out, is a direct expression of values. Similarly, the multicultural activities she incorporates serve not merely to convey information but to foster respect for differences and similarities alike.

Another value at the core of Linda's teaching is a love of work. "In Linda's class," observes her colleague Paul Biwer, "even the youngest children are learning that work is a social expression of support for the group. Work is something that will correct most misbehaviors, most selfish attitudes, most attention-seeking. The natural desire for all people is to feel good about what they do. We've distorted the value of work in our society to suggest that if you're successful it means that you've found a way to get leisure without work, that work is for somebody else to do for you."

Balancing self-reliance with group participation is an ongoing challenge that, Linda believes, begins in early childhood. Classroom activities like the rotating "professions" and visits from local heroes are two approaches to the same goal — for children "to start to see themselves as responsible citizens, even at three, four, five and six years old." She wants them to begin asking not "What can I get?" but "What is my contribution?"

On a Friday near the end of the year, the citizens of Room 7 have invited some of their favorite class visitors and local elders to a "Heroes and Sheroes Luncheon." Several parents and grandparents are present for the occasion. Patrice's great-grandmother Mrs. Heyer, age 90, has brought her 85-year-old carved wooden doll. Jerry Brown of the Kutenai/Salish tribe is back, wearing his traditional dance outfit.

"It's not a costume," he tells the children as he explains the various components. "It's real clothes."

Teddy touches Brown's braided yarn belt. "That blue stuff," he says, "is made of blankie."

In turn, the honored guests give brief presentations, while children and their families watch from a row of small chairs. Brother Nantambu, a popular local storyteller, uses a talking drum to bring alive an African tale. Dr. Rucker, the neighborhood librarian, describes her visits to five of Denver's international sister cities and displays souvenirs, including a miniature Taj Mahal. In closing, she quotes Robert Louis Stevenson's famous epigram on diversity: "The world is so full of a number of things, I'm sure we should all be as happy as kings."

Min's mom translates for Brother Pramaha, a Thai monk from the Buddhist temple Min's family attends. Wearing the bright saffron robe of his vocation, he asks the children, "Why were we born?" Then he answers himself: "We were born to practice goodness and gratitude to those around us." After his brief talk, he dips a flower in water and touches each child twice on the head to bless them.

Mr. Joe, dressed in his Sunday suit, doesn't make a presentation. He just sits in a small chair and lets kids climb on him. The children of Room 7 met Mr. Joe on one of their walks in the park. He's a retired African American man who fishes in the pond every day.

"When men are fishing," Linda says, "we expect them to say, 'Be quiet! Get those little kids out of here — they're going to scare all the fish away!' But the first time we met Mr. Joe, he was so approachable, so gentle and so kind. We all felt that we had known him for years. He's always that way. Mr. Joe meets every criterion of a hero for them. And for me."

From a "buffet" of food in the kitchen corner, the children serve their elders' plates first, then join them for pimiento cheese sandwiches, fruit and punch. A vase on each table holds a bright bouquet. "Asante sana!" the children sing in Swahili. "Thank you very much!"

For Linda Alston, the celebration of role models close to home makes an ideal end-of-school party — it encompasses all the themes she's emphasized throughout the year. But it's also a "life lesson" anyone can teach.

"This is one way of bringing back the 'African village' concept. I know it's trite now — 'It takes a whole village to raise a child.' But first you need a village."

Around the carefully set tables of Room 7, four generations and a dozen cultures share a meal.

Linda takes a moment to reflect on the scene: "The more children begin to feel connected to their community, to people around them that they can start to see as heroes and sheroes — people who are doing what otherwise might be considered mundane or common things — they will feel safer, they will feel more loved and it will be universalized. So that they'll eventually start to think, 'I met Mr. Joe and look how much he loves me. Maybe ten more people out there really love me, and I just don't know them yet.'" ★

R E F L E C T I O N 7

Prejudice Formation

A myth exists that young children, born prejudice-free, only learn discriminatory practices from negative, external sources. In fact, children naturally and consistently display prejudicial attitudes and act in discriminatory ways. However, prejudice in young children should not be viewed as miniature versions of adult attitudes nor as assertions of larger societal messages about race.

Perceiving the world through an egocentric lens, young children can respond negatively to individuals who possess unfamiliar traits. Further, they may exhibit prejudice by using negative words — such as "bad," "mean," "ugly" or "dirty" — to reject individual playmates and to express generalized judgments: "Don't play with stinky Claire" or "White people are mean." Stereotyping, on the other hand, often lacks harmful intent but may reflect limited knowledge or experience: "Indian people wear feathers."

Young children are also capable of repeating negative racial comments in context without recognizing their full significance. For example, 3-year-old Tommy, who is White, tells Ujima that she isn't invited to his birthday party because "Black people can't come in my house." Although such remarks resemble adult racist conduct, the two are not equivalent. All racially biased comments are nonetheless hurtful for young peers to endure and disturbing for adults to hear. Teachers must recognize and address the harmful effects of this behavior on both the perpetrator and the targeted child, as well as understand the implications of racial supremacy manifested in these remarks.

Scholars who examine prejudice formation in young children caution that prejudicial behavior must be understood in relation to cognitive, emotional and social development, along with children's particular experiences as members of a dominant or oppressed group (see Racial and Ethnic Awareness, p. 16). Psychologists describe how White children and children from racial-ethnic minority groups form prejudicial attitudes differently (Aboud, 1988; Ponterotto & Pederson, 1993).

While some White children express negative racial attitudes as young as age 3, it is more common for this behavior to begin in 4-year-olds. At this age, White children begin to notice the ways in which people are similar to or different from themselves. They tend to exaggerate differences in order to clarify similarities within racial-ethnic minority groups. Although they may echo adult racial terminology, their behavior often manifests a lack of understanding. For example, a White child can declare, "I hate Black people," yet refer to Black friends as "brown" and have a Black peer as a best friend.

In research settings, when asked to pick the "bad" person from a cluster of racially and ethnically diverse photos, most White children ages 3 to 5 select the pictures of Black children. They also identify pictures of Black children as the least preferred playmates. Around ages 5 to 7, two-thirds of the White children report that Asian, Black or Native children are both "bad" and disliked. Some psychologists argue that isolated studies of this nature are faulty because they do not take into account the children's interpretation of the word "bad"; nor do they prove that this description is transferable from the photo to other individuals and situations (Branch, in press).

Studies also indicate that White children's developmentally based prejudicial attitudes begin to decline at ages 7 to 8 (Aboud, 1988). At this age, most White children understand

that they and others are permanent members of racial or ethnic groups, as well as individuals with unique personality traits.
During this stage, White children are more receptive to information aimed at reducing prejudice toward racially different
classmates. However, in real-life play settings, most White children at ages 7 to 8 do exhibit preferences for other White
children as friends over racial-ethnic minority children.

The pattern of attitude formation in racial-ethnic minority
children seems to be different. Most 3- to 6-year-old Black children do not appear to have in-group preferences, nor do they
reject playmates who are different from themselves. However,
around age 7 they begin to form attachments to their own
group and become pro-Black. They develop neutral attitudes
rather than rejecting attitudes toward Whites but acquire negative attitudes toward American Indians, Asians and Latinos.
Children in the latter groups appear to exhibit the same early
sequence of attitudes and behaviors as Black children. However, around age 7 they prefer their own group and are neutral to Whites and negative toward Blacks (Aboud, 1988).

Despite these observed variations, prejudice in young children exists in all racial and ethnic groups. It hurts those who
practice it, those whom it targets and those who witness it.
Although prejudice and discrimination cannot be totally elim-
inated, teachers and parents have a responsibility to intervene
in order to minimize these elements in children's lives. While
it may be developmentally normal for 2-year-olds to display
self-centered prejudicial behavior, older children and adults
can neither develop nor sustain healthy self-concepts through
the devaluation of others.

References

Aboud, F. (1988). *Children and Prejudice*. New York: Basil Blackwell.

A P P L I C A T I O N   7

Facing Prejudice

Through the normal developmental process of learning to discern and accommodate differences, young children often exhibit behaviors that suggest prejudice or even racism. However, because young children have not internalized the ideology of prejudice, nor do they understand the sociopolitical implications of race, teachers can help prevent these early responses from developing into lasting attitudes.

Activities that affirm, value and celebrate racial and ethnic differences in the classroom context are the best ways to teach young children to accept self and others. Alert observation and sensitivity to equity issues will indicate when and how to intervene appropriately.

■ Prepare an environment that respects all racial and ethnic groups. For example:
  1 Develop lessons and use materials and resources (e.g., books, posters, music, art) that reflect both cultural diversity and human commonality.
  2 Watch for stereotypical images in classroom decorations, lessons, books, music.
  3 Support children's curiosity about racial and ethnic differences to help them understand diversity and see differences as natural and special.
  4 Provide opportunities for cross-racial and cross-gender interactions.
  5 Affirm children's home cultures through classroom resources and "sharing" of family traditions. Avoid singling

out children of color as examples or cultural carriers
for the benefit of majority children (e.g., "Mary, you're
Chinese; can you show us how to use chopsticks?").

- Take an active role against hurtful situations that occur in
  your classroom. For example:
  1 Intervene when children are excluded from play because
  of color, culture, class or language.
  2 Address children's racial comments that reveal misunder-
  standings.
  3 If a child uses a racial epithet, determine his or her understanding of the term. Explain that such words are mean
  and make people feel bad.
  4 Involve parents and brainstorm appropriate solutions
  when racial incidents occur.

- Assume accountability for personal and school practices
  that promote discrimination. For example:
  1 Examine and reflect on your own patterns of response
  toward children and adults of different races, ethnic
  groups, social classes, religions, etc.
  2 Discuss with staff members any biased actions or comments directed at young children or adults by staff.
  3 Evaluate school policies and procedures for prejudicial
  elements (e.g., disciplinary practices, staffing diversity,
  student classroom assignments, categories or lack of
  categories for multiracial students on school documents).
  4 Seek in-service diversity training for staff and parents.

R E F L E C T I O N   8

Heroes

On a daily basis, young children encounter make-believe and real-life role models. Cartoon superheroes, along with bigger-than-life sports figures and entertainment stars, seize children's imaginations with daring exploits, remarkable skills and glamorous images that defy the limitations of ordinary life. By idolizing such figures, children vicariously transcend their own perceived lack of control over the world around them. Yet these heroes often foster exaggerated concepts of excellence and may compromise young children's capacity to recognize admirable traits in others. Fixation on "superheroes" can make children less aware of the real champions in their lives.

The actions of cartoon superheroes can lead young children to think that the essence of being "super" lies in the ability and license to act in ways that others cannot control. Through role-play, children emulate these extraordinary behaviors: Super-woman chases and captures dangerous criminals; Monsterman flies around hitting everyone who crosses his path. Superhero play is often violent, repetitive and simplistic. It generally lacks the critical thinking, problem-solving and creative elements that characterize other pretend-play interactions.

Some early childhood educators advocate forbidding super-hero play; others believe that it is possible to redirect aggressive play while maintaining sensitivity to the child's interests. For example, children can play superhero games on a tabletop with miniature figures and still incorporate exciting themes such as "good versus evil" or "danger and rescue" (Beaty, 1995).

In one case study, a preschool teacher was able to diffuse the violent aspects of superhero play and yet support the child's need to feel empowered (Ayers, 1989). She humanized the superheroes. For example, she would suggest: "Let's write a book about Darth Vader's mom" or "Do you think the Phantom's kids think he's bad?"

Heroes that are commercially packaged and "imposed" on children represent a different type of role model from those that originate in folk traditions and literature. The latter are shaped by a communal aesthetic over time and endowed with lasting cultural values. Additionally, legendary heroes, such as Br'er Rabbit, La Llorana and Robin Hood, typically exhibit complexity of character and use their own ingenuity rather than superpowers to accomplish their goals.

Young children also display unbridled hero worship for real-life media icons such as Michael Jordan and Mr. Rogers. Whereas such figures embody positive traits, they are removed from children's actual lives and potentially play a limited role as mentors and role models. Likewise, historical icons such as Harriet Tubman, Abraham Lincoln, Martin Luther King Jr. and César Chávez are often presented to children as awe-inspiring adult characters in a context that is disconnected from the children's own life experiences.

Captivated by the phenomenal qualities of superheroes and historical icons, young children may fail to recognize the true heroes in their lives: a grandmother who walks a 5-year-old to kindergarten every morning, an uncle who coaches a peewee basketball team or a firefighter who saves a family's home. Attributes such as bravery, helpfulness, honesty, kindness, patience and pride are all "heroic" qualities children can learn to identify in individuals they admire and love. The task for teachers is not simply to present alternatives to media superheroes. Rather, it is to help children develop the capacity to admire true heroism in others and to recognize this potential within themselves.

References

Ayers, W. (1989). *The Good Preschool Teacher.* New York: Teachers College Press.

Beaty, J. (1995). *Converting Conflicts in Preschool.* Ft. Worth, TX: Harcourt Brace.

Kuykendall, J. (1995). "Is Gun Play OK Here???" *Young Children,* 50 (5) 56-59.

A P P L I C A T I O N   8

Supporting Children's Power

Power, danger and excitement are attributes young children commonly associate with superheroes. The resulting play — often physical and aggressive — can be redirected so that all children have the opportunity to experience power and control in safe pretend environments. Likewise, children can learn that the attributes and abilities of real heroes extend to people who surround them daily, providing valuable services that ensure their well-being.

The following activities suggest ideas for modifying aggressive play so that children can explore a variety of ways to feel "big and powerful" as well as safe and relaxed. As you evaluate your efforts, watch for changes such as broadening of interests, self-regulation of negative aggressive play with strong negotiation skills, refusal to be the victim of an aggressor, and mixed-gender grouping in superhero pretend play.

■ Engage children in activities that explore and define difficult abstract concepts such as power, control, abilities, rights and personal needs. For example:
  1 Challenge children to think critically about what makes a person heroic.
  2 Discuss with the class disturbing superhero pretend incidents that may occur, with an emphasis on how the "aggressor" and the "victim" feel, and with possible solutions that empower and affirm everyone.

■ Help children consider why some heroes are known only to

them, while some heroes are known to "everybody." For example:

1 Discuss heroes from children's immediate communities (e.g., watch for newspaper and magazine articles and tape television news segments that document heroic events) and compare them with "national" and "historical" figures such as Martin Luther King Jr., César Chávez, Dorothy Day, Chief Joseph, Aung San Suu Kyi.

2 Describe heroes that go unknown — nurses; bridge builders; volunteers who work in homeless shelters, pet shelters and soup kitchens.

■ Analyze what a role model is and discuss ways children themselves, you as teacher, and significant others in children's lives can exert positive influence. For example:

1 Have students describe people in their lives — parents, relatives, caregivers, neighbors — who have performed heroic deeds.

2 Explore ways children can be superheroes to others. Plan and execute positive "heroic activities" that extend beyond the classroom (e.g., paint a blue space in the school parking lot for drivers with disabilities to use; make small gifts or prepare entertainment for hospitalized children or residents of nursing homes).

3 Use badges, certificates or a cloth cape to reward "superhero" deeds in the classroom.

these little hands

Kindergarten teacher Mary Stewart has three voices. When she's telling a story or giving instructions or just making conversation, her usual exuberant speaking voice draws the children in. She saves her "big" voice for serious matters — like calling the class away from scattered tasks to help solve a problem. And for certain times, such as a moment of special gratitude or when the usual commotion has spun out of control, she speaks with her hands, silently.

Mary has taught her students — all hearing children — a basic American Sign Language vocabulary. She finds that communicating in sign calms them and focuses their attention. A roomful of boisterous kids, she says, will settle down to "listen" with their eyes as soon as her fingers start moving.

Each year, she begins by teaching her new class the signs for simple words like "hello," "thank you" and "goodbye." For children who tend to wait until the last possible minute, the sign for "bathroom" provides a way to leave quietly to meet their urgent needs. She gradually adds complexity, signing the words "time, eat," for example, then later inserting the preposition "to." "Time, go" becomes "time to go," then "time to go to lunch (or play or home)."

What started as a simple classroom management technique keeps branching out. "Last year, a parent was deaf," Mary says, "so when she'd come in, they wanted to sign to her. It became a little more formalized. This year, the group went wild with it." They've used take-home signing charts to teach their families. Janet's mother told Mary that her daughter signs to herself as she falls asleep.

In Mary's view, the key ingredient of her curriculum is curiosity — stimulating children to reach out to other people even through the barriers of disability and language differences and unfamiliar backgrounds. Diversity on paper, she explains, can be studied and appreciated, but it doesn't demand the personal commitment of actually talking and listening to someone who is different. Through a broad range of activities such as interviewing, consensus-building and problem-solving, she spends nine months each year helping children make real-life connections with each other and with members of their community.

"If I could wish something for every child in the world," Mary says, "it would be to feel good enough about themselves and their environment to have the confidence just to talk to the person in front of them."

Signing offers a welcome oasis of quiet, but Mary isn't out to banish noise. Most of the time, Room 3 at New Haven's Edgewood Elementary is rocking — with teamwork and talk and sometimes song. "They can sing or sign," Mary says. "Or sing *and* sign." Two songs that the kindergartners have learned "bilingually" this year are "This Pretty Planet" and "The Dream of Martin Luther King."

The decor of Room 3 is the visual equivalent of hubbub. There are low tables everywhere — learning centers holding cups of markers and crayons, baskets of blocks and clay. The medical center features stethoscopes, a blood-pressure cuff and a collection of stuffed animal patients. After classmate Nigel broke his arm on the playground, the children busily wrapped Ace bandages around teddy bear limbs.

The science end of the room has a saltwater observation tank with sea slippers, periwinkles and mussels. Bean plants sprout from paper cups. At the beginning of the year, Douglass excitedly discovered a worm on the concrete. Stewart explained that rain had flooded the worm-holes, and the children decided to make a wormery — a shelter for homeless worms. The aquarium full of dirt is regularly stocked with earthworms found on the playground.

Every inch of wall space is covered with art projects, writing samples, colorful letters. The small chairs are worn and chipped. Bookshelves and an old upright piano crowd a front corner. Not even the space on the piano lid is wasted — brightly colored Lego and Duplo projects sit there on display.

The only thing that's missing is a teacher's desk. Mary stores her personal belongings on a cupboard shelf and her guitar under a table. She never sits down except on a child's chair in the meeting circle.

All day every day, Mary Stewart — a petite White woman in her mid-30s, with long brown hair — is the eye in a hurricane of 25 five-year-olds. She has no teacher's aide, though parents and other adults frequently help out as volunteers. Twenty of her children live beyond the nearby park in a low-income, predominantly African American neighborhood. The remainder, Latino and White, live in Westville, the socioeconomically diverse area immediately surrounding the school. An array of New Haven private schools attract most neighborhood families that can afford them. Others try to get into public magnet programs. Those who are left go to Edgewood.

Principal Gerald Baldino puts a positive spin on these statistics: "To coin a phrase, we consider ourselves 'urban advantaged.' We have something to offer that the private schools don't. It's a microcosm of the real world. We really celebrate diversity."

Mary has lived in Westville for several years — just a block and a half from the school — but until last year she taught in the nearby affluent suburb of Woodbridge. A group of Edgewood parents who had seen her in action recruited her to their school.

Persuading her to leave the luxury of a suburban facility with its nationally acclaimed library, scores of computers, leafy nature trail and swimming pool was the easy part. According to parent Lorraine Rose-Lerman, "The quality of the work Mary was doing with the children was not anything you need a million dollars to do. It could happen anywhere."

The real challenge was negotiating the move with the New Haven teachers' union and a complex school bureaucracy. But the effort paid off.

"I've waited my whole life here in Connecticut to be working in my neighborhood," says Mary. "Because when I see these kids at the park or at the store, there's a connection."

She has built a bond of trust and affection in Westville and is widely known. When parents tell Mary they've walked by her house, she says, "Why didn't you stop by? Next time stop by and say hello." All the families have her home phone number.

At the beginning of the school year, Mary asks parents and guardians what their schedules and interests are. Then she works out ways for everyone to take an active role in the life of Room 3. Some want to be classroom volunteers. They choose a center to work in — blocks, art, science — and help students by making signs, showing how letters are formed, cutting out complicated shapes for art projects. Some prefer to come at night and do chores like binding and laminating children's books. Others are willing to host a field trip to their worksite or to be interviewed in class. The benefit to each child extends far beyond the parent's particular service.

The interviewing activity originated with a parent volunteer who worked as a reporter for the local newspaper. He explained to the children that they could conduct interviews just like he did. The idea blossomed. The students began by interviewing each other, then children in other rooms. Soon, anyone was a fair subject, as Mary or a volunteer escorted pairs of cub reporters around the school and neighborhood to interview teachers, family members, a store clerk, the school nurse.

"It's a process," says Mary. "They discuss questions before-hand, what they want to know about this person. And then they report back to us." The name of each interviewee in turn is added to a special bulletin board. "By the end of the year, we'll have a full board of the school community."

After months of sharpening their curiosity, as well as their speaking and listening skills, the children now invite someone new each week to visit for a group interview. Mary acknowledges that focusing 25 little minds and bodies on such an activity can be a challenge, but the shared discoveries make it worthwhile.

She recalls a recent interview with Larry Daniels, the school custodian. "When his name came up, some kids said, 'He just cleans.' I said, 'Oh, he just cleans? Well, we have a lot of parents who do cleaning. I clean when I go home.' That started a whole week-long discussion."

At Mary's prompting, the class began to observe and talk about what the custodian did for them every day and about how they treated him. Mary herself was startled to realize that every-one — including herself — routinely ignored him when he came in to empty the trash, except when they had something to add to his bag. She asked the children to consider how the bathroom got so nice and clean overnight.

In the process, Mary found her own awareness heightened. She started greeting Daniels cheerfully when he entered the room. She took closer notice of the school environment and helped the kids tune in: "Did you see the floors? He got up that big spot of paint that you put down there the other day." She took them around the school to count the number of rooms he had to take care of.

By the time Daniels came for his formal interview, Mary says, "he was a celebrity. He was this individual that kept our room going. I waited to have the interview until they had some kind of connection to him in a real way. And the very first question Nikki asked was, 'How can you clean the whole school? It's huge!' A lot of the students said, 'My parents do this at home, too,' or 'My parents go to a job where they have to do that.' By the end, no one ever uttered those words, 'It's just cleaning.'"

"Do You Care About Your Friend?"

On the first day of school this year, four children came off the bus hitting. In the first week, Mary was punched in the face twice by children who showed no remorse. This was the toughest group she had had in 10 years of teaching.

"When all the kids came in," she recalls, "they really looked at each other like they were different. Their eyes would get big, and you could tell they were nervous with each other." For many, it was their first close encounter with children of a different racial, cultural or economic background.

From the outset, Mary is clear about her expectations: that Room 3 will be more than a classroom; it will be a caring family. A basic building block of mutual respect and teamwork that she introduces right away is the daily class meeting. Early in the year, meetings work like ice-breakers, helping the children and the teacher learn about one another's backgrounds and communication styles. Later, classroom conflicts get sorted out at impromptu "problem-solving" meetings in which everyone's voice counts.

Together, Mary and her students develop a set of class rules that may be amended throughout the year. After group discussion, some of the children inscribe their own suggestions on the chart. Others dictate their ideas to Mary or a classmate. And a few illustrate their decrees with drawings or magazine cut-outs. Each household gets a copy so that everyone knows the fundamentals: "Be polite," "No hitting," "Take turns with the see-saw," and the like.

The rules are just a baseline, Mary says. More important in reducing conflict are the experiences and reinforcements that make children *want* to get along. One preventive technique emerged when she noticed how many playground spats began with put-downs. As an alternative, she introduced the "put-up," an idea she remembered reading about years ago. Once a week, she chooses someone for the class to bombard with compliments during meeting time. A spontaneous put-up session might be called to boost someone who's feeling bad.

"In the beginning of the year," Mary says, "they often compliment how kids look. Then they get beyond that." She takes every opportunity to demonstrate meaningful praise, calling attention to what someone does well or something one child did for another. "By mid-year," she adds, "a kid might say, 'I don't feel so good. Would you guys give me some put-ups?'"

As with signing, Mary finds, kindergartners enjoy mastering a repertoire of "customs" that help the class run smoothly. "This year we're doing something new that came directly from the children. Isha once said to the other children in the meeting circle, 'You really don't care about me because you're not listening to me.' The whole 'Do you care about your friend?' technique developed out of that discussion."

Now, when the children start to wriggle and whisper as a classmate shares a project or a story, Mary stops the presentation and says, "It doesn't sound like you care about your friend. Show her you care by 'sitting safe' and looking at her. Do you care about your friend?" Most often, this reminder prompts the children to refocus their attention and listen with respect.

"Can I Touch Your Sneakers?"

Sometimes a serious situation requires more detailed attention. Mary believes that problem-solving must take precedence over class work. One morning during meeting, she saw Georgia hit her neighbor, Lionel. Both children were about to cry. This was all the information Mary had to go on when she opened the floor for a problem-solving session.

"Once the meeting's called," she says, "each child has an opportunity to discuss what happened to them. If someone was hurt or hit, they are the first one that's allowed to speak. Lionel was so upset, he almost couldn't tell what happened."

But as Mary sees it, it's her job to give each party the time it takes to be heard. Lionel's eyes brimmed over. He said he just liked Georgia's new sneakers.

"They looked great," Mary remembers. "They were clean. They looked smooth. He wanted to touch them."

Georgia rebutted that he was grabbing her feet. She was scared and didn't like having him touch her.

"Her first reaction was 'whack!'" says Mary. "Lionel cried because he felt horrible. He didn't want her to think that he was grabbing her. His feelings were hurt."

Much of the conflict that Mary sees among her kindergartners is rooted in simple misunderstanding. Airing their grievances allowed Georgia and Lionel to see the sense behind rules like "Ask permission to touch someone" and "Think before you act."

Over a week of meetings, the class discussed what had happened. Days later, Mary heard students say, "Don't grab people. You might make them nervous." Now she hears, "Can I look at your sneakers?" "Can I touch them?"

Mary believes that "children naturally want to solve their problems, but some don't know how." She has consulted books on conflict resolution and peaceable classrooms and adapted and refined what works. Her methods continue to evolve.

The teacher's time-honored task of answering misconduct with blame and punishment, Mary says, fails to foster real responsibility for behavior. Under that kind of discipline, "they'll be fine as long as I'm standing in front of them, because *I'm* the discipline. I'm in charge. But the moment they leave my sight, they'll do it again because they'll never develop any inner control. I think teaching consequences — that a child's actions have an effect on others — is what's important."

This morning, Mary uses her "big" voice: "Room 3, come quickly! Sit down. We have a problem, and we need everyone's help."

The youngsters leave their work centers and scurry over to the carpet. They sit in a circle, listening carefully and seriously as the story unfolds.

"What happened, Douglass?" Mary asks.

"Marco twisted my arm," explains the tearful boy rubbing his elbow.

The teacher asks the alleged offender to explain his side or defend himself, but he doesn't have much to offer. She turns to the group for suggestions. Several hands go up.

"We only have time for ideas from two people," Mary explains, "Dougie, it's up to you to choose who you want to help you."

He points to Hannah. She offers a three-point proposal: "Marco should be nice to Douglass the rest of the day. Marco should think about what he did to Douglass, and he should sing him a song."

Mary asks Douglass if he wants Marco to sing to him. Douglass says, "No."

Next Douglass chooses Martin, who takes a firmer stance. "Maybe Marco should sit on the wall during recess or lose computer all day." The others nod knowingly — computer is Marco's favorite activity.

To bring the discussion to a close, Mary reminds everyone of the rule they made at the beginning of the year: "When we play, we don't grab anyone. It's a rule you made yourselves."

In the end, the class decides that Marco should lose his turn at computer. Since the whole class shares one terminal, loss of the day's privileges means Marco will have to wait a week for his next turn.

"They're tough on each other," Mary observes. "But this is their room. They can say, 'We don't want to put up with this.'"

Marco apologizes to Douglass and promises earnestly not to do it again. The boys shake hands. Mary signs "Thank you," and the children rush to get their coats for the playground.

Now and then, Mary does get discouraged. When she introduced problem-solving, concerned parents called to ask if their child was a "problem" or was being singled out. "For a while I was hearing from parents every night," she recalls.

After a few months, as they witnessed their children's enthusiasm for the process, they became Mary's allies, and now some even use the problem-solving techniques at home. By mid-year, three classroom moms had reported that when they and their partners argued, their children spoke up: "Don't scream and yell. I can help solve your problem."

Mary is most heartened when she sees concrete and lasting changes in behavior. A tough little boy named Mustafa is a good example. "In the beginning of the year, he wanted to hit all the time. He was unfamiliar with expressing feelings any other way." She sees the progress he has made and rejoices in his ability to control his aggressive impulses. Recently Mustafa went to the principal's office to confess that he took Joey's fruit bar out of his lunch bag and ate it.

"The secretary almost fell over," Mary says. "She asked me, 'Why did he say that?'

"I said, 'Because he knows he was wrong.'

"'Well,' she said, flabbergasted, 'I'm used to them swearing they didn't do *anything*.'"

Emmett is another child who gives Mary hope. Early in the year, as the 5th graders earnestly conducted a schoolwide "town meeting," Emmett reached up and punched Mary in the nose, for no discernible reason. She felt it would be disruptive to do anything at the moment. Immediately after the assembly ended, the children had to be hustled onto the bus to go home, but she warned Emmett that she would be calling his family the next morning to discuss what had happened.

When she called one side of his family, she got nowhere. Next she tried the other parent. No support. She moved down the list of phone numbers the children had filed and got Emmett's concerned grandmother.

The grandmother agreed to talk to him, and Mary did see an improvement in the boy's behavior. He began gradually to trust that the teacher wouldn't put him down or hit him. One day at work time he told Mary he got mad a lot because he couldn't make his fingers do some of the things the other children's fingers did.

Mary encouraged him to pick partners in class who could help him write his name and his letters. Emmett, who is Black, chose

Rosemary, a White child. She enjoyed helping and looked to him for help in turn — with overcoming her profound shyness.

At first, the partnership disturbed Rosemary's mother. She expressed concern about Emmett's reputation for rough behavior. But one positive connection can offer "problem" children a foundation to build on. To everyone's delight, Emmett has, in Mary's words, "turned into a sweetie." He and Rosemary are now fast friends.

Unexpected friendships have become a hallmark of Room 3. Mary attributes the development in part to a problem-solving meeting several months ago. "Someone was upset and said [to another student], 'I really want to play with you, but you're always with these other two people.' We're a neighborhood school," says Mary, "so if your two best friends live on your block, it's natural to want to be with them."

During the problem-solving session, someone brought up one of the songs they had learned in sign: "Make New Friends and Keep the Old."

"How about every time Mary sings 'Make New Friends,'" the child proposed, "we have to mix each other up?"

"It became a game," says Mary. "They love it now. Someone might yell in the line, 'Make new friends in this line!' and they all run around with different people. All of a sudden, their similarities and their differences become interesting. The single most important thing in teaching tolerance, I feel, is getting them to speak to each other and listen to each other — to really want to know what someone else is saying."

Boards, Hammers, Nails

Pedro, a high school senior, comes to Room 3 one day a week. He contacted Edgewood School at the beginning of the year to volunteer as part of his work/study program. He told

Mary Stewart that he played several instruments and would like to work with children in music. She was delighted to get the help.

What Pedro didn't tell her before they met was that he is blind and hearing impaired. He walks with a cane and wears a large hearing aid.

"The first thing that went through my mind," Mary recalls, "was, 'Have you worked with kids?'"

He had. When she advised him that her students might take advantage of his disability, he persuaded her to let them try.

Mary admits that the results have surprised her. "In the beginning, they were out to play tricks on him sometimes — just like they do with me. But [they learned that] just because Pedro can't see doesn't mean he doesn't know what they're doing. If someone isn't sitting, he'll know. If someone's tapping the ground instead of holding their instrument, he'll know."

The day the whole group interviewed Pedro — after he had been with them for several weeks — they mainly wanted to talk about what a great musician he is. "He just happens to have special needs," says Mary. "I didn't go out and seek Pedro. He just came to us to work with music. That's how he fits in."

Room 3 kids are accustomed to seeing people with disabilities — the upper grades have special education classes, and the neighborhood has several group homes. Furthermore, Mary points out, the "mean streets" have disabled a number of the children's relatives and acquaintances.

When a child does have questions about Pedro's blindness or his hearing aid, both Mary and Pedro give straight answers. Small-group exercises like weekly "blind art" projects help children explore their senses and practice empathy for their friend. Three blindfolded students working together on a clay sculpture learn firsthand lessons in perception and cooperation.

Mary's concern for the needs of the disabled grows out of practical necessity rather than abstract philosophy. She asks, "How do I use Pedro's skills to teach the children? How do I get someone in a wheelchair into the classroom?" And she is ever mindful of an important principle of kindergarten, "How do we make this fun?"

This matter-of-fact approach to disabilities will be getting its biggest test soon. Mary has invited her friend Rebecca Behrends, a psychologist, to Room 3 for an interview. Rebecca uses a wheelchair. Edgewood occupies an old building designed long before the requirements of the Americans With Disabilities Act were a built-in part of a school architect's vision.

A couple of weeks before Rebecca's scheduled visit, Mary introduces the problem by bringing a wheelchair to class, along with a toy one and a miniature ramp. It doesn't take the children long to figure out that the school entrances all have steps.

"We could *build* a ramp!" someone suggests. Mary, anticipating just such a brainstorm, has already begun collecting lumber. After a complete inspection of doorways, the children determine that the side entrance will be the easiest to adapt.

Years of working with kindergartners tell her that this project will require more than just physical preparation. There are mental and emotional dimensions as well. Some of the children are excited, Mary says, but "some are worried. Some are scared." When she asks them what the wheelchair makes them think of, one boy says, "My grandfather was in a wheelchair, and he died."

Mary sits in the chair and moves it around as she explains the difference between a disease and a disability. Gradually, a few children ask for a turn. When they begin asking what it's like to get around the building in a wheelchair, Mary expands on the idea. A phone call to Yale-New Haven Hospital gets things rolling: They agree to loan her four of their smallest chairs.

A few days later, Mary arranges orange traffic cones to create an obstacle course on the school parking lot. The borrowed wheelchairs are lined against the curb. In turn, each child takes a driver's seat and attempts to dodge the cones. Cries of "Help!" ring loudly as frustrated children get their wheels stuck in a small hole.

The physical and mental task of maneuvering a wheelchair is a tough challenge. Few of the students can follow Mary's instruction to pretend that their legs are wet noodles. When Daniel hits the pothole, he stands up and walks away.

When Principal Gerald Baldino comes out to observe the activity, he brings along an adolescent student. "This is Carlos. He used to depend on a wheelchair. He's an expert and offered to help." Carlos gives the children pointers on judging distances and turning. With his guidance, they all make it through the maze, chairs intact and bodies exhausted.

At their next meeting, Mary asks how the children felt trying to steer the chairs.

"It was fun!" says Emmett.

"I was scared," says Hannah, and several other children nod their heads. Some children report that they have relatives who use canes or wheelchairs. Several are being raised by older grandparents. Mary hears: "My grandmother had a stroke" and "My aunt uses a walker."

"This project is not about being handicapped," says Mary. "It's about wholeness. I want the children to look at life more whole. The handicapped are people in our community. Let's look at all of us. We're all different. We all have strengths. Let's help each other."

To assist with the week-long ramp construction project, Mary has recruited parent volunteers and another teacher. She puts together small groups of children that she knows will work well together. Mixing and matching strengths and weaknesses, she believes, is the key to cooperative learning.

Mary divides the activity into several workstations. For the ramp itself, she spreads out a sturdy plywood sheet and long triangles of wood in the middle of the meeting area. She drags out the tool crate, filled with safety goggles, hammers and a large box of nails and warns the children not to use tools without goggles. Students take turns hammering, gripping tightly with little hands. The noise is loud, and several children cover their ears even though they are clearly enjoying their jobs.

Mary, who served as a motor-pool mechanic in the U.S. Army to earn money for college, believes that children are so accustomed to high-tech equipment and elaborately constructed toys that they have little concept of how people actually make things. Using real tools gives them a new appreciation for labor.

"If you don't learn how to cut a piece of wood to mold a boat," she says, "then you don't understand what it took someone else to create that piece of work. You take it for granted. Someone said you could pre-drill those holes so it's easier. I said, 'I don't want it to be easier. I want them to know how hard it is to put that one little nail in that ramp!'"

Because many Edgewood parents work with their hands — on assembly lines, as nurses' aides or housecleaners — Mary sees her building projects as ways to reinforce family respect. "Everyone leaves this room with an appreciation of anything done physically. In our culture, we tend to have an intolerance toward anyone who doesn't work with high-tech tools, such as computers. An attitude develops that if you don't work with technical equipment you are lower class."

At another workstation, sheets of yellow and red construction paper are piled up with a neat stack of pre-cut black wheel circles. By cutting two yellow square shapes and pasting them together on red paper with generous globs of glue, adding four black wheels and a yellow handle, the children can create Matisse-like wheelchair collages.

A table with a large removable top reveals a cache of wooden blocks, wooden wheels, long dowels, short pegs, metal eyelets. Working independently, the children assemble these components into miniature wheelchairs. Then they lavishly decorate their creations with bright markers and crayons. Each resulting toy vehicle is unique. Every child is thrilled to have one to take home.

Self-respect is another byproduct Mary recognizes in hands-on construction. "Kids grow up thinking they can't do these things. When I teach basic woodworking techniques, which they can do at home, all of a sudden they are engineers, designers. They are creating things that really work and move. Sometimes they say, 'You're a mom. Moms can't do that.' I say, 'I'm a mom, and you know what? Right now my husband is home cooking, and I'm here using my tools!'"

On Friday, the measuring and cutting and hammering are over. Mary lets the children personalize the finished ramp with crayons and markers before the adults slide it into place. Everyone goes out to greet Rebecca as she arrives in her specially equipped van. She dazzles them by demonstrating the carpeted lift that lowers her onto the sidewalk. Hannah gets to use the remote control to raise the lift and close the door. Gail later reports to her grandmother, "Rebecca has a cool van."

The children line her path as Rebecca rolls toward the side door. The fresh wood of the incline is spangled with names and doodles and flowers. "I've never had a decorated ramp before," Rebecca tells her young hosts. "It's beautiful!"

Mary sticks a shiny blue "handicapped accessible" symbol on the wall beside the ramp. It's the only accessible entrance to the whole school.

As she reaches the top of the incline, Rebecca throws up both arms in a gesture of triumph. The Room 3 carpenters cheer with pride.

They sit in their meeting circle peppering Rebecca with questions. As a psychologist and mother, she is comfortable with their curiosity: How does she shop? How does she get into bed? How did she lose the use of her legs?

Calmly, Rebecca tells the frightening story of the car accident that disabled her five years ago. She reminds them to always wear a seat belt. The children are relieved to learn that her son, Justin, came through the accident unscathed in his baby safety seat and that he now attends 2nd grade at Mary Stewart's old school. Rebecca and Mary became friends when Mary taught Justin in kindergarten.

Rebecca demonstrates the kind of wheelie she has to "pop" in order to overcome sidewalks without curb-cuts. Once, she tells them, she flipped over backwards onto the sidewalk, her limp legs flung over her head. Strangers rescued her.

Mary knows why the children are quiet and thoughtful after Rebecca's story. They have experienced much in their young lives. Some have seen shootings and beatings. They understand being helpless. They're also confused. How could she allow herself to be rescued by strangers? They have heard over and over that strangers can hurt them. Rebecca quietly explains that she had no choice but to trust them.

Before she leaves, Rebecca distributes a stack of bright yellow cards. On one side, bold black letters read "Parking Violation." The other side explains that the recipient is parked either in a space reserved for the handicapped or across a wheelchair ramp. A cartoon at the bottom shows a police officer telling a driver, "No, 'Handicapped Parking' isn't for people who have trouble parking!"

Mary tells the children to keep the tickets handy. If they spot a car without the proper sticker parked in a blue space, they can leave a ticket to remind the driver about accessibility. She has lofty goals for Room 3. "I want my students to feel secure about themselves and to speak out about injustice. I'm looking for pro-active kindergartners here!"

A few days after Rebecca's visit, Tyrell, one of Mary's most challenging youngsters, was standing alone at the fence that borders the school. Two disabled men walked slowly along the sidewalk communicating in sign language. In order to sign, one of the men paused to lift his arms from his crutches. Two 4th graders began to taunt the pair.

Six-year-old Tyrell shouted at them to stop: "Why are you making fun of them? Do you know them? They're just like you. They're talking to each other." ★

R E F L E C T I O N   9

The Inclusive Classroom

Almost 50 million citizens — nearly one in five — claimed a disability in a 1991-92 U.S. Census Bureau survey. Yet most of us find the subject of special needs easier to avoid than to address. Adult apprehensiveness about the topic only thwarts children's natural curiosity, reinforcing the confusion and fear they may feel when encountering differences they don't understand. And for children with special needs, the ignorance and insensitivity of others often leads to painful stereotyping and exclusion.

Derman-Sparks (1995) describes how children develop awareness about ability differences. By age 2, children begin to express curiosity and concern about unusual attributes such as "funny talking" or the absence of a leg, as well as special equipment and other markers of disability (e.g., crutches, wheelchairs, eye patches). At ages 3 and 4, children want to know what people with disabilities can and cannot do.

Preschoolers lack a firm grasp of concepts such as permanence and change. They may wonder why a woman with a missing hand doesn't just "grow a new one." It is helpful to explain that disabilities cannot be made to simply "go away," nor is there any need to worry about "catching" someone's disability.

Teachers can point out that we all have limitations and that we find various ways of overcoming them. If we are too short to reach something on a high shelf, we use a step stool. To examine a bug up close, we use a magnifying glass. From these examples, it's easy to proceed to more specialized tools like glasses, Braille and guide dogs for the sight impaired; sign language and hearing aids for the hearing impaired; and canes, walkers, prostheses and wheelchairs for those who need help getting around. Learning about these devices as tools makes them seem familiar and normal.

The practice of mainstreaming children with diverse abilities is founded on the belief that children of all ages have the capacity to work and play cooperatively with others of varying abilities. Ideally, mainstreaming does not attempt to minimize or "erase" differences. Rather, it provides the opportunity to teach children how to respond positively to the full range of differences, including those of ability (Sapon-Shevin, 1983).

Three strategies can be helpful in fostering empathy across ability differences (Edwards, 1986). First, children should be given concrete information about the specific disability of their classmate. This will reduce fear as well as the perception of ability differences as "strange."

Second, the skills, strengths and talents of children with special needs should be pointed out so that other children will see them as peers, not objects of pity. For example, the teacher can explain, "Maria talks to us with sign language. Would you like to learn how to sign?"

Third, the feelings of all children, including those with disabilities, should be acknowledged by teachers to make children aware that everyone has similar needs for affection, comfort and fun. If Sam cannot speak, the teacher can highlight his expressive behavior: "Look at Sam smile. He likes playing with you" or "Do you notice how Sam hugs his bear when he misses his mom?"

The issue of fairness can emerge in classrooms when children with special needs require individual consideration. They may need extra assistance from the teacher or help from their peers, as well as additional time to complete tasks. For example, a child who is functioning at a lower level of cognitive development may need help matching colors, while a child in a wheelchair might have to be first in line more often. In subtle ways, teachers can emphasize that every child, regardless of ability level, has special needs. Careful attention to individual differences helps remove the spotlight from the "exceptional" child.

While teachers can employ special techniques to teach differently abled children basic skills such as dressing, sipping from a straw or reading, only children working together as friends can learn from each other the crucial skills needed to develop socially and academically. If social relationships across ability differences do not develop naturally, teachers can intervene. Children with physical or intellectual challenges might need teacher assistance to enter play groups and to sustain playtime with peers. Likewise, children who do not have special needs might need help learning how to be sensitive to the difficulties and competencies of children who do.

Through a variety of social interactions, children come to realize that everyone participates in their classroom. A classroom in which diverse abilities are represented offers endless possibilities for fostering and modeling empathy, kindness and justice. Children in such settings learn that a truly inclusive community is based not on special accommodation but on mutual adaptation.

References

Edwards, C. P. (1986). *Promoting Social and Moral Development in Young Children.* New York: Teachers College Press.

Derman-Sparks, L. (1995). "Children and Diversity." *Early Childhood Today,* 10 (3) 42-45.

Sapon-Shevin, M. (1983). "Teaching Children About Differences: Resources for Teaching." *Young Children,* 38 (2) 24-32.

A P P L I C A T I O N   9

Responding to Special Needs

As children with disabilities are increasingly mainstreamed into classrooms, it is important to facilitate their entry and to make all class members feel comfortable. With adequate preparation, young children can be very helpful to classmates who have special needs. Likewise, children with special needs can improve their social and behavioral skills in group settings where they feel good about themselves.

The following suggestions provide ways to modify and expand daily routines and curricular activities both to acknowledge ability differences and to include all class members. These suggestions presume that children with special needs are not treated with undue attention or lowered expectations. To evaluate the extent of true inclusion, observe whether an activity elicits positive contributions from all children.

■ Provide experiences that include people with disabilities as individuals, friends and citizens. For example:
  1 Use books, toys and other materials that depict children and adults of diverse abilities.
  2 Supply the necessary resources, learning materials and physical settings to accommodate children with disabilities.
  3 Invite guests with special needs to present activities in your classroom; focus on their "regular" traits first (such as job and family) and the activity they will lead. Create a relaxed atmosphere for questions and answers about disabilities and other matters.

- Incorporate information about special needs into the curriculum. For example:
  1 In lessons on the human body, explain that some people can't see or can't hear or have difficulty doing so, and that others can't move around very easily on their own.
  2 Teach children the appropriate terminology for and purpose of enabling equipment (e.g., "That 'metal thing' on Amit's leg is called a 'brace.' It helps him walk.").

- Acknowledge lifestyles of people with disabilities in all curricular areas. For example:
  1 In a communications unit, have children demonstrate non-verbal ways of conveying information and find signs and symbols that relate simple messages, then let them invent their own signs.
  2 When studying transportation, show and discuss how people with disabilities drive or ride in various vehicles.
  3 During neighborhood walks, look for landmarks that include handicapped parking spaces, Braille markings on elevators, or curb-cuts and wheelchair ramps.
  4 Use role-play to explore ability differences (e.g., cover ears and/or eyes, communicate without talking, and practice using appropriately scaled walkers and wheelchairs).

- Foster a broader awareness of and advocacy for social issues concerning people with special needs. For example:
  1 Remember that all people have the right to tell or not tell their story. Help children balance curiosity about ability differences with respect for privacy.
  2 Encourage children to be keen observers of their school, homes, stores, neighborhood and public buildings, looking for ways to make their community more "user-friendly."

R E F L E C T I O N 1 0

Play and Work

Play is the universal language of childhood, the most immediate and effective means by which children understand each other and the world. Through play, young children develop the skills and confidence required for competence in the cognitive, creative and social spheres. This "business" of childhood is also a basic right that provides its own rewards.

While children often report a distinction between play and work — play is what you "can" do, while work is what you "have to" do — their self-directed activities do not reflect this dichotomy. Pretend play in preschool, for example, often consists largely of "work" such as building, housekeeping or doctoring. And play at all levels of childhood incorporates active learning. Some early childhood programs, such as Montessori, emphasize the constructive function of play by referring to all structured activity as the child's "work."

The developmental aspects of children's play have been studied at considerable depth. Psychologists observe that children enhance cognitive skills through play that involves practice, imagination and re-creation of events. Sociodramatic play improves memory, fosters appropriate conversational behavior and increases vocabulary. The rules that govern imaginary games teach children to separate thought from objects and to exercise self-control (Vygotsky, 1978). Children also learn cooperation and conflict resolution skills through play friendships.

Research on play, however, has often lacked cultural breadth. Most U.S. studies on how children play, work and learn have emerged from a Eurocentric perspective. The impact on play of cultural variations in family values, child-rearing practices and social structures has often been ignored. Even today, racial-ethnic minority children's play behaviors are commonly measured against a dominant-culture norm.

Cultural Patterns of Play

Many of the skills that young children acquire through play reflect the particular values, child-rearing practices and social structures of their home culture. While this process does not result in identical or even predictable behavior among children of the same cultural group, it does produce patterns that can help teachers understand and accommodate variations in play-learning styles in the classroom.

Observed differences between the play patterns of White children and those of racial-ethnic minority children appear to reflect broader cultural contrasts. Generally speaking, European American culture has an individualistic, private and competitive orientation, while a collective, social and collaborative style is more prevalent in racial-ethnic minority groups (Greenfield & Cocking, 1994). These respective value systems shape both intergenerational and peer interactions, learning preferences and cognitive development. As they "learn" to play in culturally conditioned ways, children prepare for adult life in their particular culture. Not to recognize and utilize this distinctive play-learning in the curriculum is to obstruct many children's natural pathways to social and academic competence.

White and Black children's complex socio-dramatic play reflects their cultures' high regard for verbal communication skills. White parents tend to use verbal instruction to promote children's ability to play responsibly while separated from adults in social situations (Greenfield & Cocking, 1994). In contrast, many Black parents socialize their children in a collective and interdependent style. The pattern of prompting children to perform "play-talents" such as singing, storytelling or dancing for other adults reflects these cultural preferences.

Parents in many American Indian and Latino cultures also tend to socialize their children in ways that promote interdependence and unity within the extended family. For example, young Pueblo children playing with clay eventually learn to make traditional pottery pieces by watching and assisting adults. Young children in these cultures are often expected to perform household duties, thus learning to balance the world of work and play at a very young age. By the age of 5, Navajo children are often involved in sheepherding, a solitary activity performed in settings that encourage visual perception, imagination and silence (Tharp, 1994).

Studies suggest that, regardless of race or ethnicity, families with traditional means of livelihood, such as agriculture or artisanship, generally support a higher degree of play-learning in children than other families do. Thus, for example, the farming, hunting and handicraft skills of White children from traditional, rural homes originate from early work-play experiences.

Most children from Asian cultures, like their African American, Indian and Latino peers, are also socialized in a collective manner that stresses group needs over those of the individual, and readiness to cooperate rather than to compete with ingroup members. Generally, emotional maturity and compliance to norms are expected earlier in Asian children, while social initiative and verbal assertiveness are expected earlier in White children. Studies have also found that Asian mothers often prepare the play environment to support school readiness and early learning activities (Kim & Choi, 1994).

Real-World Connections

Schools can safeguard every child's right to meaningful play by providing appropriate environments, materials, time and

138

supervision, and by designing culturally responsive play-work activities within the curriculum. Through the use of real or child-scale implements, tools and work materials for play, teachers can enhance children's sense of competence and connection to the larger world. Classrooms that include resources from diverse fields of adult work offer the opportunity to counteract economic or work-oriented prejudices present in the community and in the media.

Regardless of cultural context, early childhood play offers outlets for practicing relationships, exploring emotions and mastering skills in safe, child-controlled environments. Children's good feelings about themselves and others develop through active engagement in play and work. Teachers who are able to design play-work experiences that value home cultures ensure every member of the classroom community access to the delights and benefits of play. *(See also* Gender Awareness, *p. 50;* Heroes, *p. 105; and* Little Utopias, *p. 164.)*

References

Greenfield, P. M., & Cocking, R. R. (Eds.). (1994). *Cross-Cultural Roots of Minority Child Development*. Hillsdale, NJ: Lawrence Erlbaum.

Kim U., & Choi S. (1994). "Individualism, Collectivism, and Child Development." In Greenfield & Cocking *(see above)*.

Tharp, R. G. (1994). "Intergroup Differences Among Native Americans in Socialization and Child Cognition." In Greenfield & Cocking *(see above)*.

Vygotsky, L. S (1978). *Mind in Society: The Development of Higher Mental Processes*. In M. Cole, V. John-Steiner, S. Scribner, & E. Souberman (Eds. & Trans.). Cambridge, MA: Harvard University Press.

APPLICATION 10

Integrating Play and Work

Children's earliest understandings of fairness, equity and tolerance develop in play. With close attention to the nature and extent of children's interaction, teachers can reinforce or redirect behaviors as necessary through the curriculum. Play-work activities can also reveal the knowledge-in-progress that children bring from home to school. This, in turn, will help you modify and adapt your program to provide the best services. *(For activities promoting gender equity and nonviolent play and for suggestions on preparing a welcoming environment, see* Fostering Gender Equity, *p. 53;* Supporting Children's Power, *p. 108; and* Creating a Child Haven, *p. 168.)*

■ Promote equity and respect through the common ground of play. For example:

1 Introduce children to games, dance, music and art from different cultures, particularly those represented in the classroom.

2 Provide play-work experiences that minimize competition and promote cooperation and collaboration.

3 Observe play activities in order to assess and document learning preferences/cognitive strengths and report this information to parents as part of children's ongoing progress.

4 Encourage parents and community members representing a variety of professions to demonstrate the "tools" of their work for children.

■ Acknowledge the value of children's own work and that of others through play. For example:

1 Display the evidence of "work" created through play (e.g., take photographs of elaborate structures; write anecdotal records of developmental changes in children resulting from imaginative and problem-solving play).

2 Make "play-kits" for children to take home. Include props for storytelling, play dough, Popsicle sticks, puppets, etc. Encourage children to share in the classroom what they did at home.

3 Include varied materials associated with "work" in the play areas (e.g., brooms, computers, musical instruments, work clothes, carpenter aprons, hats, briefcases, etc.).

4 Plan enough time for quality play to take place; respond to and participate in the various play/work activities (e.g., taste the imaginary rice; help cut out doors and windows in the spaceship box; admire the pottery bowls; discuss the job-well-done at the office, the hospital, the hair-dresser or the play house).

■ For more in-depth exploration of play-work issues, draw from personal as well as professional resources. For example:

1 Hold discussion groups with parents to gain information from their perspectives on play and learning.

2 Read and share with colleagues materials specific to the developmental process in racial-ethnic minority children.

3 Collaborate with other caregivers to seek, gain and provide information about play and work (e.g., consult local university experts, watch for nearby conferences, contact local and state school departments for services).

CHAPTER 6

peace takes practice

W hen Lourdes Ballesteros-Barron was an 8-year-old student at a private school in Miami, she had a teacher who would walk up and down the rows of desks carrying a heavy math textbook in one arm. Every time a student gave the wrong answer, the teacher would slam the book down on the child's head. Lourdes became so terrified of school that she spent almost every night of her 3rd grade year throwing up.

Thirteen years later, when Lourdes became a 1st grade teacher at a public school in North Miami, she was determined to make school fun. But her more experienced colleagues warned her to be stern, and she soon found out why: The 30 children she faced every day were already seasoned in the habits of hitting, pushing and calling names. As the other teachers explained it, violence was a fact of life in the children's neighborhoods.

Meeting chaos head-on, Lourdes found herself routinely pointing out wrongdoers, writing their names on the board, handing out "frowny" faces and even keeping her most troublesome 6-year-olds in detention. Every night, she went home hoarse from raising her voice.

She had wanted to be a teacher who would make children smile, but her children weren't smiling, and neither was she. In a sickening flash of insight, Lourdes understood the frustration that might have led her 3rd grade teacher to turn the textbooks themselves into weapons. The children's resistance and her own reaction had become a vicious circle. Lourdes decided she would have to find another way to teach or find another career. If she was going to realize her vision of a happy classroom, she had to dispel the established notion that violence was her students' natural impulse.

Seven years later, Lourdes is a teacher who rarely raises her voice in class, who avoids criticizing students' mistakes and who believes in the power of small children to solve big problems. Both she and her children are happy to come to school every day. She credits her own transformation and the transformation of her classroom to the training and materials she received from the Peace Education Foundation, a Miami organization whose Peaceworks curriculum of storytelling, role-playing, conflict resolution skills and "I Care Rules" is now used in more than 20,000 schools in the U.S. and Canada.

In Lourdes' kindergarten classroom at North Miami Elementary School, peacemaking is the central theme. All day long, Lourdes models the simple, specific rules of behavior that she wants her children to practice at school and at home. Story time is followed by brainstorming sessions in which students create solutions for the story characters' conflicts. During dramatic play periods, Lourdes helps children practice skills of respectful communication by re-creating typical classroom clashes, such as line-breaking or crayon-grabbing. Whenever a real conflict arises, the students involved move to the "Peace Table," where they work at putting the classroom philosophy into action.

The room itself is arranged and decorated to reinforce the message of peace. On one wall, a paper quilt of self-portraits displays each child's vision of what he or she can do "as a peacemaker."

Jacquese writes: "I will help my classmates learn."

Cassandra, who has drawn herself with a broad smile that resembles an upside-down rainbow, declares: "I can share my toys."

Others add: "I will shake hands." "I can help my brothers when they fight." "I will hug my mommy."

On the opposite wall, a paper cloud hangs over a blue and green construction-paper globe circled by children vividly clothed and complexioned. Huge letters in the cloud spell: "We are all a family under one sky!" Another poster announces: "Together, everyone achieves more," and nearby the children have drawn images of what they can do as a team: play, work, build things, put together puzzles.

Behind Lourdes' desk are posted the I Care Rules. There are five, and all the students know them by heart:

1. We listen to each other.
2. Hands are for helping, not hurting.
3. We use "I Care" language.
4. We care about each other's feelings.
5. We are responsible for what we say and do.

Student desks are configured to encourage group work, in sets of four facing each other. Each desktop features a distinctly decorated placemat displaying the occupant's name in large print. Giovan's design is a symmetrical arrangement of multicolored hearts, stars, triangles and squares. Coutchard's placemat shows stick people being transported by spaceship through a galaxy of abstract shapes.

One area of the classroom is set aside for a special purpose. The Peace Table is these kindergartner's summit site, a private, neutral setting for negotiating differences. To help with the difficult task of voicing uncomfortable feelings and listening respectfully, the problem-solvers have a menagerie of hand puppets to choose from. Two small chairs keep the proceedings simple, one-to-one. The table is covered in bright cloth and backed by a bulletin board that displays photographs of children from earlier Peace Table sessions. The photos let the children know that peacemaking is a time-honored activity here.

A New Way of Teaching

The 30 kindergartners in Lourdes' classroom come from mostly low-income Haitian and African American families. Many of these children start school having already learned that the world is an uncertain and often hostile place. A central part of Lourdes' job, as she sees it, is helping children recognize, cultivate and trust their positive instincts.

In her first year of teaching, Lourdes saw that the most benign events could be provocation for violence. "If a pencil fell from one child's desk and another child picked it up, they assumed that the child was stealing. One day, a child hit another with a rock and the boy was bleeding, and the child who hit him just laughed.

"They automatically resorted to violence, and I would raise my voice. They were negative and I was negative. It was like a war: Who was going to be tougher — them or me? These were five- and six-year-olds! I wasn't doing a terrible job of teaching; they were learning. But I was upset with myself that I was focusing so much on the negative. And their behavior wasn't getting any better."

As she searched for a way to recover her vision of school as fun, Lourdes realized that her children spent more time in school than they did at home. "I wanted to be like a second mother to them. I don't want the children to feel any fear. I want them to feel comfortable here."

In the Peace Education Foundation (PEF) program, Lourdes found some simple tools and guidelines that helped her create peace in her classroom. She discovered that peace is a never-ending process that demands constant attention and absolute commitment, but the rewards are great.

During the Peace Education Foundation's three-day training sessions, teachers like Lourdes learn that their primary challenge is not to change the children but to change themselves. Diane Carlebach, a PEF early childhood specialist, explains, "The program can only work if teachers are committed to looking at themselves. For instance, if we want children to learn how to treat each other with respect, we have to treat them with respect."

For Lourdes, treating children with respect required breaking old habits. No longer could she rely on a loud voice and the threat of detention to control the class. Though these tactics never really worked, they were such familiar responses that changing them was not going to be easy.

One of the first skills Lourdes had to learn was how to stay calm and friendly in the face of disruptive behaviors. She paid close attention to her habitual responses to trouble and practiced doing the opposite of what she felt like doing. She forced herself to smile when she wanted to glare, to speak softly when she wanted to shout, to move slowly when she wanted to rush.

"If they started going crazy, I just took a deep breath and tried to stay calm. The first change I noticed was in myself, in my own attitude. I became more peaceful within myself and more positive with the kids."

Like many teachers, Lourdes was not immediately convinced that unruly children could be taught self-control without conventional discipline techniques. The idea of doing away with punishments and reprimands sounded good, but would it really work?

In place of singling out "troublemakers," she began tallying *good* behavior. Tables of four students rather than individual children could earn points for listening, standing quietly in line, following instructions, being polite.

"Instead of 'sad' lists, they get all these points for doing the right thing. I give them stickers, but it's always for the positive. I never take anything away. And it works. They get so excited; they love the recognition. I started doing a 'thumbs up' sign, and it made them feel so good, they started doing thumbs up. And they know that we never do thumbs down. If someone does something wrong, we talk to them and help them to do it right."

When Lourdes tells other teachers about the changes in her classroom, she urges them not to take her word for it but to try it themselves. If they are consistent and persistent in their attention to the peace process, Lourdes says, they will be astounded by the changes they'll see.

Having watched other teachers put the peace principles to work, Lourdes concludes that the key to success is the teacher's willingness to try. "The teacher *has* to be the role model. Sometimes, teachers who are trying this ask me, 'When is it going to work?' and I tell them 'It's going to work as long as you do it. But you have to do it every day. And if your attitude is negative, it's not going to work.'"

Lourdes has a chance to demonstrate her new approach as she is talking to a visitor in the classroom. Her 30 students are coloring and chattering at their tables, and the longer Lourdes spends with the visitor, the louder the children get. After a few minutes, the background noise is a low roar. Then a piercing squeal is heard, and Lourdes turns quickly around to face the class. For a moment, her face reflects frustration. She doesn't speak right away but looks intently around the room.

It takes only seconds for her face to relax into a smile. "You know, you guys at Table One are doing so great, you're using your manners and being polite and you're making me so happy! Thank you!"

The room gets quiet. "Should we count our points, Table One?"

Aloud together, the students count the checkmarks beside their table number on the chalkboard and discover that they've earned 10 — enough for a happy face sticker. "Yea!" the students cheer together.

Building peace means giving children a chance to be boisterous once in a while. Lourdes asks the class to stand up and sing one of their favorite movement songs. They jump up, clap their hands over their heads, turn around and around. The song's refrain is, "Whatever way I move, I do it in a very safe way." Two boys knock into each other and one falls down. When the song ends, Lourdes speaks very quietly. "It makes me sad if somebody is silly and doing something that is not safe. I know you don't want to hurt yourself or hurt your friends."

Lourdes routinely refers to the students as "your friends." When Sapphire can't find an eraser and becomes frustrated, she complains to her teacher. Rather than finding an eraser for her, Lourdes suggests that Sapphire ask a friend to share theirs. One of her tablemates offers Sapphire an eraser, and Lourdes articulates the lesson they have demonstrated: "See, when we ask our friends, they help us."

Listening for Solutions

The idea of helping and asking for help is a theme that will come up again and again throughout the day. And at story time, they will talk about it in some detail.

The tales that occupy story time in Lourdes' classroom are chosen specifically to teach peacemaking skills. After reading stories like "The Three Billy Goats Gruff" or "The Little Red

Hen," Lourdes leads a role-play and discussion about how the characters in the story could have solved their problems.

By imagining solutions to problems in familiar stories, even very young children can begin to view themselves as problem-solvers. "They see that there is something wrong and that even though they are just five or six years old, they can make it better," Lourdes says.

After reading "The Three Billy Goats Gruff," Lourdes draws her children's attention to the life-or-death problem that the billy goats face: In order to find grass to graze on, they must cross over a bridge where a threatening troll lies waiting to eat them. "How could the billy goats solve their problem?" she asks, and the kindergartners offer their suggestions:

"The goats could help the troll find some other food."

"They could take him to the store."

"They could take him to McDonald's."

"They could invite the troll to their house and cook him dinner."

"They could build another bridge."

"They could build a boat!"

Finally, one child suggests: "The goats don't really need to go anywhere. They could just stay there and wait for the grass to grow."

Lourdes shares the children's pride in their creative thinking. Adults usually underestimate the power of children's imagination to help them solve problems, she says. Through discussions and role-play exercises, children begin to develop the skills and confidence to resolve routine classroom conflicts: pushing, line-breaking, grabbing someone's crayon, stepping on a classmate's shoes.

"In the beginning, our goal is to identify the problem, rather than blaming or tattling," says Lourdes. "They know that when I say, 'What's the problem?' they should talk about the problem instead of talking about the person."

So they learn that instead of shouting "He took my crayon!" in the role-play situation, they can keep the peace by saying calmly, "That was my crayon." Lourdes stresses that most offenses are unintentional: "Did he know it was your crayon? Maybe you can explain that to him."

They talk about how important peace is, not just in their classroom, but in the world outside. "I encourage them to think about the future and tell them that they will be responsible in the future for what will happen. I let them know that even though they're five, when they grow up, they can be anything they want. But if they don't learn to talk about problems now, they won't be able to solve their problems when they grow up."

In this classroom, there's no pretending that grownups are better problem-solvers than children. Sometimes they talk frankly about bad examples that adults set. "We talk about what we see on the news, the violence. We talk about how grownups go to jail for shooting each other over silly problems."

Sometimes the violence comes very close to home. "Not long ago, there was an eighth grader who shot another child because he was bothering him after school, and we talked about that."

The world doesn't have to be this way, Lourdes tells the children. As they learn how to solve problems peacefully, they can take those lessons home and practice them with their families, neighbors and friends.

"They see they have a reason to learn to solve problems both in the classroom and at home. And they learn that the I Care Rules are not just rules for kids but are good rules for everybody."

The I Care Rules are the core of the Peaceworks curriculum. Typically, they are first introduced through a hand puppet, the "I Care Cat," who explains what they mean and demonstrates how they are used.

The I Care Cat comes with a package of materials supplied to PEF-trained teachers that also includes storybooks, posters, activity sheets and lesson plans. The use of the cat puppet strengthens children's involvement with the I Care concepts, explains PEF's Diane Carlebach. "For children, the I Care Cat is such a nurturing and accepting entity. It's like magic. The cat comes in and teaches the I Care Rules — which are so simple — and they listen. And when they use the cat puppet at the Peace Table, it gives children the language they need to express themselves."

At story time, discussions often begin with the children pointing out that someone is not following the I Care Rules. In the case of the Little Red Hen, the talk centers on the requirements of friendship.

The children quickly become familiar with stories like "The Little Red Hen," but in Lourdes' class they always find new ways to think about the tales. As their teacher once again reads the first few pages, the children listen as if for the first time. The Little Red Hen wants someone to help her plant seeds to grow wheat to make flour to bake bread. "'Who'll help me?'" she asks in a rather demanding tone.

And all of her friends decline. The children eagerly recite the uncooperative characters' responses in unison: "'Not I!' said the cat. 'Not I!' said the dog. 'Not I!' said the duck."

They let their teacher read Ms. Hen's hmmphy "'Then I'll do it myself!'" and offer their loudest chorus yet for the final declaration: "And she did!"

Just as they enjoy repeating the words they've learned by heart, they take pride in knowing the familiar lesson of the story, which Lourdes stops occasionally to reinforce. "How do you think Little Red Hen feels?" she asks.

"Sad," says George, "because they're not going to help her plant her wheat or water it or cut it or help her take care of it."

But Little Red Hen doesn't get away with martyrdom in this classroom. She has a responsibility as a friend, too.

"What could Little Red Hen say to the cat, who was too busy eating to help?" Lourdes asks.

"Please stop eating the apple," offers Jacquese in a soft voice.

"Did the Little Red Hen ask the cat to stop eating the apple?"

"Noooo!" they all answer.

Lourdes turns the page. "Let's find out if she learns to talk to her friends."

When, predictably, all of Ms. Hen's friends reappear just as the bread emerges hot from the oven, the children scrutinize the situation again.

"Why didn't Little Red Hen want to share her bread? Those were her friends!" Lourdes asks.

"'Cause they didn't help her do nothing!" Jason offers.

They decide that, while Ms. Hen's decision not to share her bread might be technically fair, it isn't very nice.

"So what's the Little Red Hen's problem?" Lourdes asks. "She has a big problem."

Her problem, in fact, is one of the biggest that children can imagine: She has no friends. Hen's rejection of the others, though she could justify it in theory, had miserable results. The children would advise her that it's fine to have fresh bread, but it's better to have friends to share it with.

Certain that they have the solution, the children take turns enacting various ways that Hen could have kept her friends by asking respectfully for help and sharing her bread.

Speaking through cat and dog puppets, the children demonstrate how friends ask friends for help. The exercise helps them practice the language of peace with problems that don't involve them personally, so that when real conflicts do arise, they will have an idea of the alternatives available to them. Lourdes points out that they are following I Care Rules and using I Care language.

"Once we start talking about it, and we role-play and I read them stories, they get the whole concept of caring and the I Care Rules. I don't want kids to memorize them like class rules, I want kids to live by them, to go home and implement these rules in their house."

The more people in a child's life who are practicing peace, the quicker a child learns to make and keep friends, Lourdes says. She introduces parents to the process early. "I have an open house and send home a list of materials and the I Care Rules. I suggest they hang them up in their house, and I encourage them to use the rules at home."

She tells parents in very specific terms what the rules will mean about their child's life at school. "I tell them I don't allow hitting. A lot of parents tell their children that if someone hits them, they should hit back. I let parents know that I don't allow hitting back. Sometimes they get upset, but I tell them about the Peace Table and show them how it works. Later on, they see children using the I Care Rules at home, expressing their feelings more and not fighting as much. They see it working, and they start using them, too."

Gina Blanchard, the mother of two of Lourdes' former students, was 5 when she arrived in Florida from Haiti. Her parents, like many other refugees, believed that America offered a chance for prosperity and safety. And like many, they found that violence and poverty too often go hand-in-hand on the streets of South Florida. When her daughter Regine brought home the I Care Rules from kindergarten a few years ago, Gina was eager to try them herself. Since then, her second child has had Lourdes' class. "Now when we have problems we know how to talk it out instead of fighting," Gina reports. The rules don't always work, but they do offer a constructive alternative to hurtful habits.

Among skeptical parents, the word has spread that the peace strategy can change patterns of behavior. After her daughter Paula had Lourdes' class, Alina Capuozzo requested that her younger son Joey be assigned to Lourdes when he was ready for kindergarten. Joey was a sensitive child who took offense quickly and could become overwhelmed with anger.

"When he didn't get his way, or he wanted something and couldn't get it, he'd just stand there and clench his fists like he was going to explode," Joey's mother remembers. And sometimes he did explode, pushing and hitting other children. Alina says she felt Lourdes could help her son control his emotional outbursts.

The help Joey got came mostly from other children, Lourdes remembers. "A lot of times Joey had a hard time expressing himself. The kids knew that when he got angry, he didn't want to be touched. They knew there was a special way of helping him, and two of them would lead him to the Peace Table and then leave him alone for a little while. Then they would go talk to him."

By the end of the year, Joey discovered that he had options when he was angry. And Alina has seen the difference in his behavior. "The other day he was telling me that someone in school was teasing him because something fell out of his book bag. I asked, 'What did you do?' I thought he'd gotten in trouble again. He said, 'I turned around and ignored him.' In the past, that would have been impossible. He would have pushed the kid down without thinking about it."

Kindergartners respond well to the idea of rules. They have strong notions of right and wrong, fair and unfair, and they are quick to spot violations. The rules help them identify such violations and address them appropriately. Once the rules become commonplace in the class, the children themselves enforce them.

"It's funny," Lourdes notes, "because they start to see differences between how kids act. They see the way other children play on the playground, and they play rougher, and the way they speak is rude, and they don't want to share. They'll come up to me and ask why, and I say, 'Why don't you teach them? You know how to be a peacemaker; why don't you help them?'"

The Peace Table

Conflict is, of course, inevitable. While the I Care Rules provide broad parameters for appropriate behaviors, children still need specific help in dealing with hurt feelings and unfairness. When a conflict arises in Lourdes' classroom, her typical response is to ask the children involved, "Would it help if you went to the Peace Table?"

At the beginning of each year, Lourdes introduces the Peace Table and the children talk about what peace means. On the wall is posted a list of their definitions: "Peace means to love everybody in the class," wrote Jacquese. "Peace means playing together," wrote Serge. "Peace means don't throw garbage on the floor," wrote Julio. "Peace means don't kill anybody," wrote Samantha.

Lourdes explains the purpose of the Peace Table to a visitor: "The Peace Table is somewhere you feel comfortable, where you can talk to your friends if they do something that makes you sad or mad. It's close to my desk, because they're more comfortable there. It's away from the rest of the class, but they're not alone, and they're close to the [pet] rabbit, too. It's a friendly place."

Posted at the Peace Table are the Rules for Fighting Fair:

1. Identify the problem.
2. Focus on the problem.
3. Attack the problem, not the person.
4. Listen with an open mind.
5. Treat a person's feelings with respect.
6. Take responsibility for your actions.

To help them learn how to use the Peace Table, Lourdes invents role-plays at the beginning of the year, first with hand puppets, then with children themselves going to the table. "I might say, 'Let's pretend that's your toy and Billy has it.'" When children first go to the Peace Table, Lourdes helps guide their discussion, in tones the rest of the class cannot hear. "I ask 'What's the problem?' Usually the first thing they say is 'Why? Why did you do that?' They know not to blame or to interrupt. I emphasize that no one is in trouble. We always say we want to know the truth so we can solve our problem."

Then, to shift the focus from problem to solution, Lourdes asks, "What do you think you could do to be happy?" She repeats their responses, checks for agreement and sends the children back to their places. As the year goes on and the procedure becomes more familiar to everyone, classroom conflicts require less and less of the teacher's time. Children take matters to the Peace Table on their own. Or they ask another student to mediate for them. Lourdes stresses, "They know it's always OK to ask for help."

The ordinary traumas of daily life for 5-year-olds provide Lourdes with plenty of opportunities to help children negotiate their disputes. As she is talking to a visitor, the children are drawing pictures of animals at their desks. Out of the corner of her eye, Lourdes sees that Danielle is crying.

"What happened?" she asks.

"Brittany turned my picture around," says Danielle, pointing to the girl across from her. "I had it like this and then she did like this," she demonstrates.

"Did you ask her why she did that?" Danielle looks down at the table and shakes her head "no."

"Would you like to go to the Peace Table and talk to Brittany about it?"

They both nod, then get up and walk to the table, where Lourdes helps them get started: "What are you going to ask Brittany?"

Danielle looks at Brittany and asks, "Why did you do that to my picture?"

Brittany is silent. Lourdes prompts, "Did you want to see her drawing? Did you want to look at it?" Brittany is now eager to explain: "I just wanted to look at her house."

"You can tell Danielle that," says Lourdes. "I'm not mad at you. We're just talking about it."

"I just wanted to look at your house," Brittany says, softly now, to Danielle.

"Does that make you feel a little bit better?" Lourdes asks, and Danielle nods.

"Did you know that she just wanted to look at your house?"
"No."

"So maybe next time what can you do, Brittany?"

Brittany replies: "I could ask her to let me look at it."

"So you can agree next time to ask her?"

Both girls nod, then hurriedly return to their seats.

The whole process, from offense to resolution, takes only a couple of minutes.

Later, the children are gathered on the floor for a class discussion, and Lourdes glimpses a ripple of conflict. She directs her gaze at two children who are arguing in whispers.

"Would you like to go to the Peace Table, George and Cassandra? Would that make you more comfortable?" In her voice, "going to the Peace Table" is as benign a notion as going to the water fountain, and the two children rise without hesitation.

George and Cassandra talk through their differences, then sit quietly for a moment until another child comes to the table and asks if they're finished. They both nod, and all three return to their seats, where the class discussion has continued without interruption. It is not necessary for Lourdes to investigate what the problem was or how it was solved. Between 5-year-olds, she says, altercations are frequent but easily forgotten. Given the tools, children can solve most conflicts on their own.

But when they are no longer small and the dangers they face are greater, will they still know how to wage peace? Their chances are best, PEF specialist Carlebach believes, if peace education is implemented throughout the school years. "It's a process, and it works for the teachers who use it, but it would be so powerful if everyone was following the I Care Rules."

In Palm Beach County, the Peaceworks curriculum was implemented in every school in 1993 as a way of addressing system-wide school violence. Younger children learn the basics, while older children learn specific conflict resolution techniques and more complex decision-making skills. Already, the results include a sharp reduction in fighting and suspensions, but administrators are particularly excited about what the program will mean for the youngest children. Students who entered kindergarten in 1993 or later could spend their entire public school careers in classrooms where peace is all-important. Administrators believe that those children can make a huge difference not only in their schools, but in society at large.

Long-term goals aside, the small steps honored in the I Care Rules offer their own immediate rewards. For Sonja, a 5th grader who has been in the program from the beginning, the reason for peace is simple: "It just feels better."

Lourdes still thinks sometimes about her 3rd grade teacher. She is content that her own students will remember her year with them as a good time. When Regine, now 11, considers what she liked best about kindergarten, she recalls, "We played games. She taught us a lot of stuff about I Care. We sang songs and listened to stories. Every day was fun." ★

R E F L E C T I O N   1 1

Classroom Rules & Discipline

Maintaining a safe, friendly and consistent social environment in the early childhood classroom is a multidimensional process. Classroom rules serve as the explicit framework for this endeavor by openly encouraging certain behaviors and discouraging others. Classroom discipline, on the other hand, is the teacher's active response to conflict between children's behaviors and established goals. Positive discipline programs often incorporate conflict resolution techniques to promote responsibility and self-discipline in children and thereby reduce the need for teacher intervention.

Three factors contribute significantly to the "tone" that rules set in the classroom: (1) the process by which rules are developed, (2) the manner in which they are expressed and (3) the way they are enforced or reinforced. Rules presented as a fixed, imposed code of behavior for children to learn and follow often support an authoritarian role for the teacher. Involvement in the rule-making process, even if only to the extent of discussing and "adopting" teacher-derived rules, gives children a vested interest in their community and provides a starting point for the collaborative creation of the social environment.

The most basic rules address issues of safety, both physical and emotional (e.g., those governing hitting, climbing or name-calling), and are thus non-negotiable. Yet even safety rules contain ideas that can be expressed either positively or negatively, depending upon the desired classroom tone. For example, "In our room we respect each other's bodies" and "No hitting" are versions of the same rule, expressed in the first instance as a goal and in the second as a boundary. In either case, it remains the teacher's responsibility to terminate unsafe behavior when it does occur. Rules that promote social harmony and care of materials (e.g., those that define turn-taking or room cleanup) vary more in content, expression and implementation.

The creation and implementation of rules in the early childhood classroom raises important developmental issues. Familiarity with a rule does not guarantee that a young child understands its function or is able to generalize from one application of the rule to another. "You know we don't run in the classroom" has no meaning the moment a child decides to chase a peer who took his favorite hat from the make-believe box.

Children instinctively behave in ways that preserve their sense of well-being. Sharing is not useful to a 4-year-old when there is only one truck, and she wants it; sitting still, listening and waiting for a turn may seem irrelevant to a child who has something important to say at Circle Time.

Enforcement of rules commonly entails an immediate response to a specific act. Time-out, for example, is widely perceived to be an effective disciplinary action for routine misbehavior. Yet this short-term solution does not model, coach or reinforce positive social skills. Further, it fails to address possible cultural, racial or economic factors in both the teacher's expectations and the child's resistance. For example, a teacher who expects Black boys to be "rowdy and undisciplined" may correct them more severely and frequently. This action, perceived as unfair by the boys, can initiate retaliatory behavior judged unacceptable. In turn, the teacher may view the continuation of this behavior as the child's problem, rather than the product of child-teacher interaction.

When family socialization patterns do not match the norms of the teacher — typically White, female and middle-class —

the potential for classroom conflict increases. Consequently, boys in general and racial-ethnic minority children and children of poverty experience a disproportionate share of disciplinary actions (Polakow, 1993; Sheets, 1996). These actions, in turn, can provoke recurring patterns of resistance and coping behavior.

Factors viewed as deficient or different in the child's life, such as home disciplinary practices, socioeconomic status and cultural values, may serve as easy targets of blame. For example, a teacher who prefers quiet, well-mannered children may react more negatively to an unkempt, loud boy whose single mother never attends school functions than to an equally noisy but well-dressed boy from a two-parent middle-class home.

Defining and creating the classroom conditions needed to minimize disruptive and uncooperative behavior are more challenging and often more rewarding than the enforcement approach. Research on discipline shows that in order to reduce the occurrence of conflict, teachers need to: (1) understand why conflict occurs, what conditions exacerbate it, and how to judge behavior as acceptable or unacceptable; (2) believe and expect that all children can display developmentally appropriate behavior; and (3) comprehend how children process rules and why they choose to comply, adapt or resist (Sheets, 1996).

All teachers face situations in which children are uncooperative, angry, moody or manipulative. However, children can learn to adapt and modify their behavior if caregivers provide consistent support at home and at school. Successful teachers understand that punitive actions such as public chastisement and exclusion from the group often accomplish little more than accentuating the imbalance of power between the teacher and the young child. A more equitable goal is to help children develop the self-discipline necessary for being fair-minded and caring individuals.

References

Polakow, V. (1993). *Lives on the Edge: Single Mothers and Their Children in the Other America.* Chicago: University of Chicago Press.

Sheets, R. H. (1996). "Urban Classroom Conflict: Student-Teacher Perception: Ethnic Integrity, Solidarity, and Resistance." *The Urban Review* 28 (2) 165-183.

A P P L I C A T I O N   1 1

Encouraging Self-Discipline

In classrooms where the cultural backgrounds, family life and individual attributes of all children are respected and affirmed, teachers, children and families can collaborate to develop behavior guidelines that benefit everyone. Exemplary classroom discipline programs also take into account the developmental level of young children and emphasize modeling, coaching and reinforcement of desired behavior over punishment for infractions.

The following activities are designed to help teachers promote self-discipline in young children. As you adapt these activities to your particular needs, evaluate your program's success by monitoring changes in interpersonal conflict on the one hand and classroom cooperation on the other.

■ Involve children in establishing a positive classroom climate that includes mutually acceptable rules and guidelines. For example:

1 Develop class rules and behavior contracts through consensus and discussion.

2 Discuss how "grumpy" and uncooperative behavior affects everybody.

3 Create "Peace Tables" where children can work out their own conflicts.

4 Role-play conflict situations and include a variety of ways to solve problems.

5 Incorporate social skills as part of the curriculum and allow time for practicing them.

■ Assume that all children have the capability and the desire to demonstrate positive behavioral patterns. For example:

1 Examine how the beliefs, values and social conventions of diverse cultures are reflected in your classroom rules, procedures and policies.

2 Keep a tally on how frequently and severely you discipline members of various groups and look for patterns in how and why you determine behavior unacceptable.

3 Provide opportunities in the daily routines and activities that allow children to exhibit "good" behavior.

4 Construct activities that build trust and respect and encourage cooperation in child-teacher and child-child interactions (e.g., make "cooperation punch" or soup or salad, participate in group art projects, sew a quilt).

5 Change membership in assigned groups frequently and allow children to choose their own groups to encourage them to "practice" their developing social skills.

■ Incorporate comprehensive, coordinated strategies for children who are "at risk" behaviorally. For example:

1 Work together with families, churches and available community services to create a multidisciplinary team to achieve long-term goals (e.g., coordinate behavior guidelines, rewards and consequences; emphasize the role of caring adults in the child's life).

2 Design and implement nontraditional family support programs for children whose parents find traditional services intimidating or confusing (e.g., reading classes for parents with low literacy, English classes for native speakers of languages other than English, transportation options for parents who have transportation problems, or evening conferences for parents with conflicting work schedules).

REFLECTION 12

Little Utopias

The physical environment that classmates share is a critical resource of the early childhood curriculum. Before the children even enter the classroom, it is the teacher's job to create an appropriate setting for work, play and the practice of equity, respect and tolerance. While no amount of "design" can substitute for caring, nurturing relationships, thoughtful attention to concrete details can enhance these essential interactions.

For the classroom community, the room itself serves as a model town or neighborhood. The obvious parallels are plentiful: Children's desks or table spaces, storage cubbies and nap cots, along with kitchen and toilet facilities, provide the comforts of home. "Public" spaces such as play areas, reading nooks, bulletin boards and art displays are miniature versions of the park, the library, the billboard and the museum. Some classrooms contain window-box "gardens" and tabletop "zoos."

Beyond the obvious considerations of safety, cleanliness and comfort, the constructed environment has psychological and emotional dimensions, as well. A model neighborhood is pleasing to the eye, easy to get around in and distinguishable from other neighborhoods. A place with a strong "sense of place" promotes pride in its inhabitants and cements their group identity. And with its rich textures of use, modification and loving care, it also affirms their unique needs and preferences as individuals.

Any neighborhood — big or small — can convey clear messages of exclusion or acceptance, rigidity or adaptability, fear or friendliness. Here, the classroom neighborhood has a distinct advantage over most full-fledged ones: a benevolent designer who ensures that the environment welcomes, accommodates and nurtures every member of the community. In small ways, the teacher's decisions about classroom design can offer a vision of Utopia.

The layout of furniture within the classroom space reveals much about how the resident community works. Many primary classrooms today have abandoned the traditional "linear" organization in favor of clustered desks or work tables, with learning centers reflecting a high degree of flexibility in the curriculum.

Research suggests that an "open" arrangement promotes peer equity in a number of ways (Hallinan, 1976). For example, popularity appears to be more evenly distributed in open than in traditional classrooms. A flexible room plan is also more accommodating to variations in children's learning styles and physical needs. And when conflicts arise, the open setting seems to offer greater opportunity for independent problem-solving.

Certain standard features such as play and reading areas explicitly address the social significance of classroom layout. Within these settings, teachers can arrange major elements to enhance children's interaction. Placing the block or construction area next to the kitchen or dress-up area, for example, can encourage cross-gender and nonstereotypical play.

The neighborhood model offers rich possibilities for cultivating particular social and emotional skills. A "Welcome Center," for example, may provide opportunities for practicing hospitality toward new classmates or invited guests. A park bench might furnish a "Quiet Corner" for private reflection. A "Peace Table" can lend structure and importance to resolving disputes.

An infinite variety of objects and materials "flesh out" the basic spatial design into a classroom ambience. Posters, dolls, artifacts and multilingual signs are obvious tools for emphasizing cultural pluralism. Items that reflect the home cultures, parental occupations and shared history of class members promote a sense of belonging and provide reference points for building relationships. As classroom neighbors customize their work spaces or cubbies with decoration, they express their individuality, discover group diversity and develop "pride of ownership." By extension, teachers can include diverse examples in any category of classroom materials — such as chairs of various sizes and shapes, or blocks made of different kinds of wood — to enrich children's conceptions of similarity and difference.

Research indicates that some kinds of play resources are better than others at promoting positive social behavior. Pairs or groups of children playing with miniatures like doll houses and toy trucks, for example — which "concentrate" control over a small domain — appear to experience relatively high levels of peer conflict, while those playing with child-scale or full-size objects like dress-up clothes and workshop tools seem to interact more freely. On a larger scale, play structures that permit simultaneous use by several children, such as climbers or big boxes with multiple openings, are conducive settings for cooperation and sharing (Pelligrini and Perlmutter, 1989).

According to some studies, outdoor play is inherently more prosocial than indoor play. Freedom of movement, dispersion of boundaries, and assocations with lore, legend and animal life encourage children to create collective games and fantasies. The natural world may be the most inviting, exciting and equalizing environment of all, but it is not always available. By using natural objects and materials to add a suggestion of "wilderness" to the classroom neighborhood, teachers can foster children's shared sense of enchantment and wonder, nurture their aesthetic capacities and instill an awareness of responsibility for their common ground, both inside and outside the classroom walls (Frost & Talbot, 1989).

The rich, welcoming classroom environment is a training ground for community living. Mutual delight in the beauty, diversity and mystery of their surroundings provides a natural bridge for children's delight in each other.

References

Frost, J. L., & Talbot. (1989). "Magical Playscapes." *Childhood Education*, 66 (1) 11-19.

Hallinan, M. T. (1976). "Friendship Patterns in Open and Traditional Classrooms." *Sociology of Education*, 49, 245-265.

Pelligrini, A. D., & Perlmutter, J. C. (1989). "Classroom Contextural Effects on Children's Play." *Developmental Psychology*, 25, 289-296.

Smith, P. K., & Connolly, K. J. (1980). *The Ecology of Preschool Behavior*. Cambridge, UK: Cambridge University Press.

A P P L I C A T I O N   1 2

Creating a Child Haven

The classroom setting conveys strong messages to children about how they are regarded and how they should regard each other. What teachers omit is just as important as what they include in student materials, visual displays and physical arrangements. The classroom environment that centers the child in the learning and teaching process uses children's cultural knowledge, provides opportunities for positive interpersonal interactions, enhances a sense of community, and fosters respect among children and teachers.

The following suggestions are designed to help you construct a nurturing, culturally relevant learning environment. Periodic evaluations of your classroom climate will allow you to make necessary changes.

■ Promote a sense of ownership and responsibility for classroom space by involving children in the decision-making process when arranging classroom furniture or designing visual displays. For example:

  1 Discuss with children how furniture arrangements can encourage or discourage rough-housing, create quiet and active spaces, and enhance small- or large-group activities.

  2 Ask children to help identify types of activity areas and determine the location, content and duration of classwork displays.

■ Model inclusion and collaboration throughout the classroom design process. For example:

1 Display posters, bulletin boards and decorations that reflect a wide variety of interests, abilities and cultures.

2 Label pictures, objects and artifacts in a variety of world languages.

3 Make all work and play areas equally appealing to boys and girls.

4 Make all areas accessible to children who are physically challenged.

5 Create "Welcome Centers" for guests, and display lists that promote acceptance, respect and caring.

■ Be resourceful in bridging home, school and community. For example:

1 Include songs, stories and artifacts from children's homes.

2 Display real photos of children and families.

3 Use community resources such as tourism posters and postcards, local products and public library materials so that children can make connections from school to home to community.

layers of meaning

Here and there along the avenue, the windows of old stone row houses display potted plants, colorful curtains and lamplight. Interspersed with these signs of life are shattered panes, gaping doorways and nailed-up plywood sheets. Graffiti climbs the walls like dead vines.

In the shadow of an abandoned 16-story apartment building (one of a half-dozen public housing facilities ordered closed in Chicago's Oakland neighborhood 10 years ago) sits a little four-room school. A plain, institutional exterior belies the oasis within, where bright clean corridors and classrooms hum with the vitality of 68 preschoolers. The State Pre-K Demonstration Center is so cheerful and well cared for, in fact, that one visitor recently opened the front door, glanced around and said, "I'm in the wrong building. I'm looking for a *public* school."

For the past seven years, it's been head teacher Liz Hurtig's business to defy expectations. At a time when budget crises dictate "leaner and meaner" programs nationwide, she scrimps to retain the services of a child psychologist. As an alternative to bureaucracy and formality, Hurtig offers harried parents a couch to "crash" on. And instead of despairing at the neighborhood's chronic poverty and violence, she justifies her optimism one hug at a time.

The Demo Center, as it's called for short, was established in 1986 to showcase quality practices for prospective and experienced teachers and others who work with young children. Since 1990, the staff has committed itself to celebrating diversity, eliminating bias and nurturing relationships based on mutual respect.

The goals of this exemplary program begin with the development of children's "emotional literacy," or capacity to recognize and deal with a wide range of feelings in themselves and others. Social skills such as group play, sharing and problem-solving build on this inner foundation. And, concurrently, the exploration of similarities and differences among classmates as well as among cultural groups fosters the children's sense of both individual worth and connection to a larger world.

Demo Center teachers make self-scrutiny a part of the daily routine, regularly taking stock of their classrooms and their thought processes for signs of stereotyping. With the help of consulting psychologist Holly Johnston, they continuously monitor what Liz Hurtig calls the "emotional climate" of the school. They set aside one lunch period each week for a focused discussion of classroom concerns. Whenever possible, they take part in anti-bias workshops around the city. Hurtig, who has been teaching for 25 years, adds, "I often say that what we're demonstrating here is that we have a lifetime of learning to do."

Students at the Center — predominantly African American, with Arab American and Latino minorities, representing four Chicago neighborhoods — are children identified by state criteria as being at risk of failure in elementary school. By the age of 3 or 4, many of them are already familiar with harsh realities that most people only see on television.

Four-year-old Cedric came into teacher Cathy Main's room one day anxious to tell a story. The night before, he told his classmates at Circle Time, his dad took him riding in the car. His dad's friend was in the front seat, Cedric and his mom in back. Cedric's dad and his friend were drinking and smoking reefer. The cops started chasing them, so his dad got on the expressway and drove really fast. His mom was yelling, "Stop! Stop!" Finally the cops pulled them over. They yanked his father out of the car and threw him onto the hood. Then they cuffed him and dragged him to the police car.

"He described the whole incident in detail," recalls Main. "The end of the story was, 'And then my mom had to drive the car home.'"

Over the next few days, Cedric spent his free time re-enacting the chase in a "car" made of four chairs. His classmates took turns pretending to drink and drive, smoke marijuana, pull each other from the vehicle. "All the kids wanted to experience it and have their turn," says Main. "They rotated being the cops and the driver, and some of them had it down pat. They would put a block on the floor for the gas pedal."

She realized that her first impulse — simply to terminate the frightening and overstimulating behavior — was not necessarily the most constructive response. But neither her training nor her instincts offered a better solution. So she took the problem to psychologist Holly Johnston. Johnston proposed that Main intervene as the "good guy" by explaining, "I'm here to be the family protector. I won't let this family drink and drive because that's not safe."

The strategy turned the play around. At Main's suggestion, the thrill ride became a drive to a pizza place, an amusement park, a bowling alley. The accompanying emotions that had troubled Cedric seemed to lose their treacherous edge. But Main wonders if the messages of such an activity really sink in.

She has noticed that "for the kids who come from more violent homes, there is a difference in how they interact with others and what methods they use to solve problems. They know what they're supposed to do to conform to this environment. When I say to them, 'What should you do when someone snatches your toy or hits you?' They say, 'Use your words. Tell them I don't like that. Tell the teacher.' They have all the pat answers, but when something happens to them, when they get angry and frustrated, they can't do it because their home environment is so overwhelming."

Play scenarios like the expressway chase, says Hurtig, "give us an incomparable window into the child's concerns. Cedric's play showed us how scary it is to children when the adults they count on to protect them are themselves in danger."

Safe and Secure

Deneita Jo Farmer, whose room is across the hall from Main's, feels that teachers cannot overemphasize the basic message of security and trust. "Kids this age need to know that there is somebody who will keep them safe," Farmer says. In the expressway incident, "the police came to keep them safe. In this place, it's the teachers."

Last year, after hearing several children in her class express their fear of police officers, Farmer invited an African American policeman who had a son at the school to come and talk to them. For the first visit, she asked him to wear his "at-home" clothes. By the time he came again, in uniform, the kids knew the caring person behind the badge.

The increasingly random hazards of contemporary life, however, can shake the credibility of such assurances. Liz Hurtig thinks the recurring nightmares of inner-city schools and parents became palpably real on a national scale with the Oklahoma

City bombing in 1995. Says Hurtig, "I think what happens is adults are not convinced they *can* keep kids safe. But — until they rebuild that confidence — they have to say they can."

When conflict arises in the classroom, Cathy Main's initial response is to find out what's happening, to determine whether anyone is hurt, and to identify and affirm the feelings of each party involved. Getting the children to recognize each other's feelings is an extension of the same process. "I might say, 'Look at her face. Her face is angry.'"

Pointing out the connection between inner states and their outward expression helps to cultivate both personal responsibility and empathy for others. A poster in Laura Lopez Campbell's room displays 21 multicultural faces labeled Scared, Anxious, Surprised, Lonely and so forth, with the caption "All feelings are OK. It's what you do with them that counts."

Amidst an array of upbeat signs and artwork on Deneita Jo Farmer's walls is a photograph of a crying girl. Its purpose, Farmer says, is to suggest that the so-called negative emotions such as anger and frustration and fear are nothing to be ashamed of.

"The child in that picture happens to be a White girl," says Farmer, herself African American. "I used to have a picture of an African American *boy* who was crying. That image was very important to one of my children. Ricardo was angry about a lot of stuff and didn't know how to use language to express his feelings. But when he felt like he needed to hit somebody or curse at somebody, I told him he could go get that picture and bring it to me, and then I would help him. This year, when we look at the crying girl and talk about why she's upset, it helps the children bring up their own issues."

As Farmer and her colleagues see it, the ebb and flow of private emotions governs all aspects of classroom activity, from individual behavior to social interaction to learning and fun. One child's inner turmoil that goes unaddressed, or merely gets stifled, will eventually affect the whole group.

Stress, Hurtig points out, is an inevitable part of human development. Difficulties for young children may arise from such seemingly innocuous events as the arrival of a new sibling, a long family vacation or a parent returning to work. The more responsive teachers can be to the feelings that underlie behaviors, the more skillful and confident children can become in navigating their own ups and downs.

In cases of emotional trauma, which these teachers see frequently, the challenge is more acute. At another preschool, 5-year-old Jeffrey might be considered the classic bully. He commandeers his classmates' toys and tricycles. He uses "power language," talking back to adults and calling other children "wimps" and "sissies." He resists lying down at nap time but is usually the first to fall asleep. According to Farmer, "He uses so much energy, he's exhausted."

A child like Jeffrey can exhaust a teacher's patience as well, but Farmer remains focused on the bigger picture: Last year, Jeffrey's sister, Natasha, was wounded in a drive-by shooting.

"I think that situation impacts on every single thing he does in the classroom," says Farmer, "and probably every single thing he does in his life." Her hope is that the small moments of positive connection she tries to bring about will have a cumulative effect to help counter the trauma.

"When he gets angry and starts to snatch and push, and I can intervene, I think it has a direct relationship with what happened to Natasha. First of all, he has to think about how the other child is feeling. When the other child verbalizes that, and I help Jeffrey think about other ways to express his anger, this lets him know that what happened to Natasha is not the way we solve problems."

In addition, hearing Jeffrey talk about his sister at Circle Time — and hearing the teacher respond — helps the other children put his behavior in perspective. Familiarity with each other's lives outside of school extends the ties of community.

While the policy of open discussion sounds healthy in theory, the teachers repeatedly question its limits: How much "outside reality" can we safely allow in? Liz Hurtig notes that "crossing the threshold away from home at the age of three or four, when you're so vulnerable and dependent, is a tremendous act of courage." Kids may see firebombs and body bags on television at that tender age, but should they be allowed to hear their classmates' firsthand accounts of such horrors?

Cathy Main recently faced this dilemma when she noticed that several children were pretending to shoot each other. "At group time, I decided to talk about guns, hoping that they would come to the consensus that we don't even want pretend guns in our classroom, that guns aren't safe. What happened was they began telling me whose dads had guns, where each gun was, and when they saw their dad using that gun. I was overwhelmed."

Another revealing aspect of the discussion was the fact that it *was* a discussion. "Up to that point," Main says, "I had not been able to get this group to sit and discuss anything. But this time they actually sat and were intrigued by what each other had to say. They were comparing notes. It was a topic that went on for 15 or 20 minutes.

"I remember feeling, 'Do I stop this? Do I keep going?' and not knowing what to do, because there were a couple of kids who were very frightened by the conversation. They didn't have guns in their home, couldn't understand about having guns in the home. I felt very uncomfortable for them, but I didn't know where to draw the line."

Main sought the advice of a more experienced colleague, Deneita Jo Farmer. "Dee-Dee suggested that sometimes it's good to stop a discussion with the whole group but let the kids who still want to talk about it bring it up again later in private. That way they still have an opportunity to vent those feelings."

Psychologist Holly Johnston seconds that advice. She frequently leads small-group discussions among children troubled by or preoccupied with violence, death and other disturbing issues. One girl in a current group routinely makes playdough people and then cuts them to pieces.

"Not only are these kids being exposed to an intense, chaotic violence in their world at home," Johnston says, "but almost universally they're being exposed through TV. They're overstimulated, confused about what's real and isn't real. They don't have the wherewithal to defend themselves against it, much less to make sense of it."

Occasionally, teachers find their own defenses shaken. Liz Hurtig remembers one fall morning a few years ago. As the children filed into the building, teacher Laura Lopez Campbell pointed to 4-year-old Kamal, getting out of a woman's car. "I just found out that's not his mom," Lopez Campbell told Hurtig. "That's his aunt. His mom died a year and a half ago."

"But he's always talking about 'Mom,'" Hurtig said.

Lopez Campbell said she had just told the aunt the same thing: He's always talking about "Mom."

The aunt had explained, "We felt so bad about it that we told him she was at the store, but we never told him she was dead. When I leave, Kamal says, 'Where are you going?' And if I say 'I'm going to the store,' he says, 'Will you tell Mom I said hi?'"

Still astonished by the revelation, Hurtig recalls, "With that sentence, Laura [Lopez Campbell] teared up and put her hand out, and I teared up and took her hand, and I thought, 'Let me out of here.' I don't get that feeling very often. We each took a tissue and a deep breath, without saying anything. She walked back down and was there for those children again."

The teachers arranged for a social worker to help the family. "They were able to accept help," Hurtig says. "Some aren't." With professional counseling to help with their grief and with guidance on child development issues and communication skills, Kamal's family learned that, in the long run, the truth is less damaging than deception.

But the process was slow. Every morning for weeks, Hurtig remembers, "Kamal would come in with no look on his face — no pain, no anger, nothing. I would watch, and by the time he reached the other end of the hall he would have a smile. Sometimes you have to make do with that to keep going."

Common Denominators

At the community literacy center where head teacher Liz Hurtig volunteers several hours a week, an elderly African American grandmother browsed through a stack of newly donated books. A children's book about a Black family caught her eye, and she studied each page carefully. Turning to show Hurtig one of the illustrations, she said, "Somebody finally found out how to draw *us*."

That change was a long time coming. "When I grew up," teacher Deneita Jo Farmer recalls, "there were no Black people on television. There was no Black literature that I knew of. There were no Black children in the books that were presented to me. I had no Black dolls. I want an African American child in my class to be able to say, 'This little girl in this book has beads in her hair just like I do.'"

Liz Hurtig believes that seeing themselves and their personal experience reflected in art and literature helps children develop their sense of identity and belonging. "Skin color isn't the only attribute we need to acknowledge in the curriculum," she says, "but that goes a long way toward saying there's a place for every-one here."

Multiculturalism at the Demo Center emphasizes first and foremost the diversity within the school family. The current eth-nic mix is roughly 55 percent African American, 35 percent Latino and 10 percent Arab American — no White children attend this year. But such numbers are deceptive, says Farmer. She considers it a mistake to lump children into broad categories like language group and race.

"Culture is defined in so many ways. All African Americans are not the same. Children growing up on the South Side of Chicago are different from children growing up on the West Side. Family structures are different. Neighborhoods are different."

Hurtig and her staff are careful to avoid the "multicultural tourist" approach that, however well-intentioned, often verges on stereotyping. A common temptation for teachers, in Hurtig's view, is to use isolated artifacts to impart bits of information about different cultures. She feels that piecemeal exposure does little to build cultural knowledge or cultivate a true appreciation for diversity. Nor, she adds, does the practice make much sense from a developmental standpoint.

"Young children," Hurtig says, "are so focused on finding out who they and their friends are and what their families are like. If you have a friend in preschool whose family is a little different but a little the same, that's a real, concrete issue. To talk in an abstract way about what a child does in Japan doesn't serve this age group."

Deneita Jo Farmer makes sure that the pictures and objects in her classroom do not emphasize the "foreign" or "unusual" but rather reveal common denominators. Instead of highlighting cultural differences, she treats them as variations on familiar themes. On the wall of the housekeeping area, for instance, there are photographs of people around the world preparing food and doing other chores. The music shelf features well-worn percussion instruments — maracas, finger cymbals, a rain stick — that attest to the universal love of rhythm.

She tries to resist using cultural overlays — events, materials or themes intended to "cover" a whole segment of the population. "I take it from the standpoint of the individual person. I may play a jazz tape and let the kids know that one of my favorite jazz artists, Najee, has brown skin, and here's a picture of him." But she won't use his music as part of an isolated lesson on African American culture.

By talking about culture as an aspect of real people's lives, Farmer hopes to show children that many things they do at home are also forms of cultural expression, both different from and similar to those of other families. She envisions her classroom as a place where not just individual children but all of their home cultures can mingle.

Three years ago, when the first Arab American children came to the school, their families maintained a very formal, reserved manner toward the teachers. This year, Farmer reports, "the mothers are so comfortable that they've brought feasts in to share with us." Four-year-old Abdul found true common ground among his classmates when he declared his dislike for certain traditional dishes his mom had made and then gleefully pointed out his favorites.

On several occasions Nina, an African American mother, has come in to bake banana bread in the school oven. For Farmer, the lessons of such an ordinary act are simple but profound. "This is something she does at home with Harold all the time. Here is a Black woman who is promoting this sense of family, while society would suggest that she's not supposed to do that because she had children early, or she's on welfare, or whatever. But here is a mom who has hot cookies and chocolate milk for her kids when they come home from school, and her skin is very brown."

Early childhood teachers, Farmer believes, have a unique opportunity to "immunize" children against stereotypes before they take hold on young minds. By exposing children to the similarities and differences that all people possess, she hopes to prove that blanket assumptions about any group are unfair.

At an earlier job in a Head Start program, Farmer was told by her coordinator that she should have play food stamps in the housekeeping area instead of play money, because food stamps were what the children would be using in real life. Farmer refused. "I told her I wanted to expose this group of children to something besides the stereotypical view that all they see is food stamps. I want them to understand the currency system so that they're not limited when they get out into the world. I can't box kids up like that."

Farmer considers childhood stereotyping a natural process gone wrong — an unhealthy extension of the labeling and pigeonholing that all children use to map their world. "Young people look at things by classifying and categorizing. They begin to say, 'I'm Black, she's White.' They come to me and say, 'You're White,' and I tell them, 'No, I'm a fair-skinned Black person.'

"Sometimes I hear a child say, 'I don't want to be Black. I want to be White.' I try to find out how they view themselves, what the child understands about being Black or being White. Whoopi Goldberg does this skit about wanting light skin and long blonde hair when she was a little girl. She would fasten a sweater around her head and let it flow down her back, and that would be her hair. I can remember doing that.

"When I started doing my anti-bias work several years ago and started looking at who I was as an individual, I came to realize that I didn't know much about where I came from and what it means to be a Black American.

"I started thinking about why I'm glad to be me, and it led me to develop this very rich library of children's literature and books particularly by African American women, a collection of artwork by African Americans. That is something I'll leave to my children when I leave this Earth.

"I want kids to know that they're special, that they matter, that there are adults like them, who have the same skin color and same hair, that also matter. It helps to promote a sense of cultural pride: 'I know something about me. Now I'd like to know something about you.'"

Learning to respect oneself, Farmer says, is a prerequisite for learning to respect others. The process can require some *un*learning, as well. "If they use a derogatory word, like 'nigger,' I'll stop there and say, 'Do you know what that means?'" Usually, she finds, they don't. "Then I explain that it's a hurtful word that some people use when they're mad. But I tell them, 'Instead of using a word like that, you can talk about why you're mad.'"

The process of learning to talk appropriately about differences calls for a willingness to experiment. Liz Hurtig, whose heritage is European Jewish, recalls the experience of being described by students a few years back. "I had a whole classroom full of African American kids. One of them said, 'She White,' and another kid said, 'No. She light.' I don't think they were really thinking about exclusion or inclusion at all. They were just observing something. But I was touched."

Joyce Acker, the teacher next door to Farmer, emphasizes that there is often a considerable gap between what young children understand about race and what they say about it. Acker, who is African American, had a White boy in her room whose favorite place to sit was her lap. Yet one day he refused to hold a Black classmate's hand because, he said, "I might turn black."

Another time, the White child told the African American assistant teacher, who was wiping the tables with disinfectant, that "Black people don't use that." From parent conferences and home visits, Acker learned that some family members openly expressed bigoted views in front of the child.

When students bring prejudices from home into the classroom, Hurtig advocates a pragmatic but respectful strategy: "We may be able to say to the family, 'Some of the feelings that you express in the presence of your child are putting that child in some jeopardy at school.'" This approach works, she finds, because, rather than alienating parents with criticism, it provides a meaningful incentive to evaluate and modify their own behavior.

During breakfast at school one morning, Deneita Jo Farmer reminded Alia, who is Iranian Muslim, to skip the sausage because it was made from pork. When Jasmine, the daughter of immigrants from Ghana, asked, "Why don't you eat pork sausage?" Alia replied, "You eat pork because you're Black."

"This wasn't a stereotype," says Farmer. "It wasn't to say, 'All Black people eat pork.' Alia's not sophisticated enough intellectually to suggest that. It was to say, 'We're not the same in one obvious way, so it must connect with this other way we're not the same.'"

Whenever a moment like this arises, Farmer uses simple questions to explore the tricky concepts of similarity and difference. "This is something we continue to discuss. There was even a suggestion that maybe we need to have a breakfast table where there is no pork and another where there is pork. But the goal of that would be to stop the conversation."

In Liz Hurtig's view, any hope of helping children avoid the pitfalls of prejudice requires a burning fascination with how they think. While a statement or an action may defy adult logic, "teasing out" the ideas behind it can reveal surprising connections.

Laura Lopez Campbell, who is second-generation Mexican American, uses Spanish with several of her students from non-English-speaking families. One African American boy is especially interested in the fact that there are two languages being spoken in the room. One day he was working a jigsaw puzzle that had geometrically shaped pieces rather than the usual irregular ones. After examining the array of circles, triangles and squares, he said, "This is a Spanish puzzle."

Lopez Campbell couldn't detect anything Latino-looking about the "Sesame Street" characters the puzzle depicted. She asked him why he'd called it that.

The boy traced his finger along the straight edges and perfect curves. "Because it's different," he said.

Gray Areas

A couple of years ago, Liz Hurtig got a call from a parent who was angry that her daughter had come home from school with paint on her clothes. Never mind that the paint was water-soluble. From now on, the mom said, the child was not to participate in painting.

Hurtig couldn't imagine saying to a child, "You can't paint." She knew that the school-issue plastic smock didn't cover as much as an adult's shirt would. But she knew better than to suggest that the mom send one. Asking an upset parent to do *more*, Hurtig has learned, is a bad idea. The best policy for a teacher, she says, is to "set aside your own reactions and quick fixes and simply listen."

Paint on clothes was not a new issue in Hurtig's experience. "But this woman was so highly emotional," she recalls. "I said to myself, 'I'm not understanding something here.'" It took several conversations for the real concern to surface. One day the mother told Hurtig, "If she [the child] looks dirty, she's no good."

Despite the staff's extensive diversity training, this single statement stopped them in their tracks. Here was an issue the guidebooks didn't cover, yet a problem as simple as dirty clothes made the anti-bias concept come alive.

"I grew up working-class," Hurtig says. "My dad was a Baltimore cab driver, so I sometimes make the mistake of thinking that I can readily identify with our working-class families, even if I'm not working-class right now. *We* didn't feel that way about getting dirty. But some people *do* feel that way."

A few years ago, she points out, it would have been possible for a Demo Center teacher to react harshly to this mother's complaint, not to listen to all of her concerns, not to discover that she herself was attempting to protect her daughter from a stereotype.

Hurtig urges, "If we can somehow ally with that parent instead of becoming adversaries, we just might be able to do something together for the child." In this case, the mom agreed to let the girl continue painting as long as she wore one of Hurtig's husband's shirts and cleaned up more carefully.

"I'm as sure as I can be about paint," Hurtig says. "I'm not so sure about some other things. If you just read about these issues — 'Be open to all views' and so forth — that's easier said than done."

One matter currently under discussion is that of holiday celebrations at school. Every December, Deneita Jo Farmer's heart goes out to all the children whose parents are too poor or dis-spirited to buy them Santa Claus presents. For a long time, her own emotional response to the issue reinforced her assumption that the secular observance of Christmas is appropriate for the classroom. "I was going to be the one to save the world," she remembers, "and provide Christmas for all my little children who couldn't celebrate it at home."

Liz Hurtig recalls her own parents "doing Hanukkah in a Christmas garb," so low-key festivities at school didn't strike her as a problem. The dozens of Christmas trees in the offices of the Chicago Board of Education suggested a similar attitude among school administrators. As a courtesy, the teachers asked the Muslim families for their opinions, and none objected. Some Jehovah's Witnesses parents asked that their children be excused from any Christmas activities.

When Hurtig and her colleagues began examining their holiday policy as part of their anti-bias program, they made some discoveries that challenged their own best intentions. Jehovah's Witnesses, they learned, receive strong group support for asserting their beliefs at school or at work. Cultural and personal factors prevent many other people, however, from taking issue with authority figures. Some, for example, respect the teacher's opinion as the last word. Others fear that parental "interference" will put their child in a vulnerable position in the classroom.

Closer parent-teacher relationships gradually revealed that many Muslim parents did object to the school policy but were reluctant to say so, and that some of the African American families didn't observe Christmas either. But the decision has not been to eliminate holiday celebrations altogether. Particularly for young children, Hurtig believes, cultural observances help maintain continuity between home and school.

Now, the teachers approach the issue in a much more open-ended way. At registration, they ask each parent, "What kinds of things do you celebrate in your family?" And throughout the year, students share special occasions like Ramadan, Christmas, Kwanzaa and birthdays not as teacher-directed, official observances but as opportunities to learn about one another's lives.

As the holiday issue suggests, teachers at the Demo Center find that their work with children entails many more ambiguities than certainties. Liz Hurtig observes, "It would be nice if in training they would say, 'We're going to make this sound very simple and straightforward. We're going to give you activities to start and finish. But once you go in the classroom door, you're going to see gray areas, and we'll be here to discuss these gray areas. The gray areas you see will be different from the ones I see.'"

"Reflection is the ingredient that's lacking in the education of teachers," says Laura Lopez Campbell. "There's no value placed on that in the system. There's no time in the school day for teachers to come together." The weekly lunch meeting is an adaptation she and her colleagues work hard to preserve.

As Harold's mother, Nina, sees it, "This school is like an extension of our family. I can come in and help out. I can come and talk to Dee-Dee about my problems. As a parent, you think you have to have all the answers, but you don't. Sometimes you just have to say, 'Baby, I don't *know*.'"

Hurtig emphasizes that no one has all the answers. "We know we don't know things. But I'm convinced that there are no skills that teachers can't learn if they're motivated to learn them and provided with the training opportunities. We're all still in this field because we've managed to hang on to the belief that one person *can* make a difference." ★

REFLECTION 13

Childhood Losses

One of the most painful lessons of childhood is that we sometimes lose things that we love. Childhood loss comes in many forms: Relocation to a new country or a new city separates friends or family members; a classmate becomes seriously ill; a grandmother dies; parents divorce; a drive-by shooting cripples a neighbor. Whether they experience such stresses firsthand, witness the grief of friends or observe traumatic events through the media, all children sooner or later feel the emotional pain that accompanies actual or perceived loss.

Teachers learn of children's stressful experiences in a number of ways: by listening to their stories, by communicating with their parents, or by observing physical or behavioral signs. Although traumatic events themselves are beyond the teacher's control and often difficult to talk about, an honest, caring response serves not only to comfort children but also to reinforce their connection to the classroom community.

Children are able to withstand profound hardships as long as there is at least one caring adult who helps them through the transition period (Cohn, 1996; Greenberg, 1996). Some child development experts maintain that the most valuable contribution teachers can make is being a consistent, nurturing and responsive adult in children's lives.

When a loved one dies, children may be disturbed more immediately by the behavior of others — disruption of routine, emotional display, unfamiliar rituals — than by the death itself. Confused about cause and effect, children may think that something they said or did caused the death or that, by association, they or other loved ones also may die.

Children ages 3 to 6 often think death is reversible or that it is only a deep sleep. They may express curiosity about what happens after death. Since children often interpret adults' explanations literally, clichés such as "Your grandfather has gone on a long trip" serve only to delay the grieving process. Children are able to experience grief as they grasp the idea of death's permanence (Goldman, 1996).

Profound loss of any kind can compromise a child's sense of security, belonging and self-esteem. The presence of physical or emotional violence, for example, parental illness or depression, family breakups and other stresses can evoke powerful, unfamiliar feelings of sadness, anger and guilt that affect children's behavior and perception of their place in the family and the classroom community. Close observation and careful listening will alert teachers to signs of emotional pain, which can include changes in eating habits, attempts to get attention, and withdrawal. Any suspicion of abuse should, of course, be reported to the proper authorities.

The grieving child's classmates may also experience a range of troubled emotions in response to their friend's distress. A teacher's acknowledgment of these feelings and expression of concern may offer a valuable emotional anchor. Just as it is important not to ignore or diminish children's grief, teachers should be equally careful not to overreact. Age-appropriate facts can be aimed at fostering compassion rather than alarm. For example, "Shaundra's mother died today. Shaundra is staying with her grandmother. She is OK and she knows we miss her. When she comes back to school in a few days, she'll need all of us to be her friends." Without sufficient knowledge, children may imagine a far worse scenario, and, with incorrect information, they often sense that they are not being told the truth.

No caregiver can protect children from all trauma and loss. But when these realities strike, the school community can be an important source of support. Open, age-appropriate communication about stressful events can help young children develop into compassionate, helpful and hopeful individuals.

References

Cohn, J. (1996). *Raising Compassionate, Courageous Children.* Atlanta: Longstreet Press.

Goldman, L. E. (1996). "We Can Help Children Grieve: A Child-Oriented Model for Memorializing." *Young Children,* 51 (6) 69-73.

Greenberg, J. (1996). "Seeing Children Through Tragedy: My Mother Died Today — When Is She Coming Back?" *Young Children,* 51 (6) 76-77.

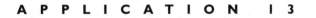

Coping With Loss

A teacher's best resource for helping children deal with loss is open communication with families. If the home support system is weak or part of the problem, teachers can work with staff specialists to seek outside help. Grieving, frightened children have to be encouraged and supported to return to classroom life. This can be accomplished through dialogue, play and work.

The following activities are designed to reduce the fears associated with emotional trauma in the classroom community. Careful observation can help teachers balance children's need to express feelings with their right to privacy.

■ Explain carefully and simply the nature of the tragic event being experienced and the emotions involved. For example:
 1 Reassure children that it is natural to feel sad when someone we love moves away, becomes sick or injured, or dies.
 2 Discuss death as a natural part of the life cycle.
 3 Ease children into discussions of their own or classmates' experiences of loss by providing relevant information and responding to their questions, perceptions and concerns.

■ Focus on the grieving child in ways that promote inclusion and acceptance. For example:
 1 "Return" the child to the class by assigning a special task such as feeding the fish or choosing a group activity.
 2 Allow grieving or traumatized children to talk about their feelings, but provide other outlets if discussion disturbs classmates. Use art or puppet play for more private expression.

3 Provide opportunities for the children to commemorate loss through play and work activities, such as making memory gifts, planting a flower or tree, lighting a candle or creating a mural.

■ Emphasize children's power to exert a positive effect on other people's lives and on the larger community. For example:

1 Conduct class discussions about a classmate's serious illness in the child's absence to focus peer concerns into constructive caring.

2 Help children create and send letters and drawings to a sick or sad friend, or collect food and other donations as gestures of compassion.

3 Encourage pretend play that allows children to practice the emotional skills of empathy and sympathy (e.g., role-play taking a friend to a hospital or welcoming back to school a peer whose pet has died).

4 Discuss how children can take action against violence and hatred by choosing not to watch certain TV programs or by selecting toys that are not associated with violence.

R E F L E C T I O N 1 4

New Visions

The purpose of this book has been to explore the multiple layers of feeling, knowledge and skill that underlie equitable, culturally sensitive work with young children. Some teachers, as we have seen, possess a natural gift for accommodating children's similarities and differences. Others intuitively seek guidance as challenges arise. In many cases, however, children's school experiences of acceptance or rejection, equity or bias, and cooperation or conflict depend on the vision of classroom community that teachers acquire in pre-service programs. Few institutions hold as much potential for positive social change as those that prepare new teachers.

The one attribute traditionally considered indispensable for effective early childhood teaching is caring. The assumption often follows that a caring teacher will create opportunities for play, learning and self-expression that serve children's present developmental needs and future school success. In this view, pre-service programs provide the intellectual and practical framework necessary to support the teacher's instinctive concern for each child's well-being.

The preceding stories suggest that this familiar model is incomplete. As essential as caring may be, it is not sufficient to guarantee every child equal importance and equal access to the teacher's expertise. Neither does the amount or quality of knowledge teachers gain in education classes ensure that their best intentions will equitably serve each child.

Preparing educators to meet the needs of children of diverse backgrounds and experiences requires more than increasing "multicultural" course requirements (Sheets & Hollins, in press). Such content knowledge, while fundamental, becomes meaningful only when it helps teachers promote acceptance, equity and community in their own classrooms. The most effective pre-service programs go beyond the caring-plus-knowledge formula to instill in their graduates the habit of continual reflection — on themselves, on the children and on the curriculum.

Teachers who strive to support the positive development of children's identities and relationships must first be willing to scrutinize their own self-image and its potential influence on classroom life. Some preparation programs offer special courses in psychology to assist new teachers in developing healthy responses to their racial-ethnic heritage. Research suggests that self-acceptance is essential for responding positively to the race and ethnicity of others (Helms, 1990).

A related approach is to enlist trained psychologists or counselors to engage pre-service teachers in individual or small-group discussions about a broad spectrum of identity components, such as race, ethnicity, gender, sexual orientation, ability, language and religion. By examining the "filters" through which they view critical diversity issues, teachers can take deliberate steps to prevent any such perspective from harming a child. The teacher's response to differences in any of these dimensions in a child or a family can nurture or hinder the child's formation of a healthy identity.

Another essential step in the reflection process involves recognizing that the world outside the classroom — mainstream U.S. culture — in many ways perpetuates a hierarchy of physical and social traits, valuing the light-skinned over the dark-skinned, the affluent over the underprivileged, the able over the disabled, the familiar over the different. Despite ongoing efforts to realize the equity promised in our national creed, many institutions that prepare new teachers likewise suffer from a limited vision of community.

For example, programs that draw heavily from the works of European psychologist Jean Piaget on child development may leave the impression that his "classic" theories apply universally to all children. In the predominantly White middle class world of early childhood instruction, teachers may expect children from other cultural backgrounds to hide their home learning in order to master an unfamiliar style without adequate assistance or even recognition of this arduous task (Hollins, 1996).

It is arguable that the growing number of racial-ethnic minority children in U.S. schools would be most equitably served by a corresponding increase in racial-ethnic minority teachers. While role models are vitally important, such a solution fails to address the crux of the problem for culturally diverse classrooms. Through inclusive, relevant preparation and rigorous, ongoing self-scrutiny, any teacher, regardless of group identity or affiliation, can develop the capacity to interact constructively with any child.

Increasingly, early childhood teacher education affirms the interpersonal nature of teaching and learning — that is, that the classroom community flourishes only as each member values every other's unique wealth of attributes, experiences and ideas. Sometimes patterns that begin as small circles ripple outward. In the face of widespread inequity and intolerance, the early childhood classroom can be a place of quiet revolution.

References

Helms, J. E. (1990). *Black and White Racial Identity*. Westport, CT: Greenwood Press.

Hollins, E. R. (1996). *Culture in School Learning: Revealing the Deep Meaning.* Mahwah, NJ: Lawrence Erlbaum.

Sheets, R. H., & Hollins, E. R., (in press). "Teacher Preparation: Embracing the Centrality of Racial and Ethnic Identity in School Learning." In R. H. Sheets & E. R. Hollins (Eds.), *Racial and Ethnic Identity in School Practices: Aspects of Human Development.* Mahwah, NJ: Lawrence Erlbaum.

bookshelf

O n the pages that follow, you will find annotated resource lists focusing on diversity education in early childhood settings. The first list, Bookshelf Basics, features 10 exceptional titles to help you in creating a curriculum and environment that promote peace, tolerance and community. Following Bookshelf Basics are additional lists that are organized thematically. These resources expand upon ideas presented in the classroom profiles and related sidebars. Each list also includes suggestions for literature to share with children.

You'll find that the Bookshelf categories listed below are not rigidly defined. Since many of the themes are interrelated, there is considerable overlap in the resources' contents, as well as in their usefulness for dealing with various issues. Also, the lists are not intended to be definitive; rather, they offer a starting point for helping children to develop positive self-concepts and to appreciate differences.

Bookshelf Basics

The books listed here are essential resources for any educator interested in teaching young children to understand, respect and value differences. They offer an overview of the key issues in tolerance education and provide guidance in creating a caring, cooperative and inclusive community of learners.

Alike and Different: Exploring Our Humanity With Young Children, edited by Bonnie Neugebauer, is a volume of reflections and illustrative stories by early childhood educators. The authors draw on their classroom experiences as they honestly address a range of subjects, including meeting the needs of all children, staffing with diversity, learning from parents, living in a changing world and evaluating multicultural resources.

National Association for the Education of Young Children (NAEYC)
1509 16th St. N.W.
Washington, DC 20036-1426
(800) 424-2460

Anti-Bias Curriculum: Tools for Empowering Young Children, by Louise Derman-Sparks, encourages teachers to celebrate diversity in meaningful ways and actively challenge stereotypes and prejudice. In this definitive text, Derman-Sparks addresses children's concepts of race and culture, similarity and difference, and disability and gender identity. "Self-check" and "caution" boxes highlight areas of particular sensitivity; other sidebars suggest ways to create and assess anti-bias environments and activities.

NAEYC
1509 16th St. N.W.
Washington, DC 20036-1426
(800) 424-2460

Geneva Gay's *At the Essence of Learning: Multicultural Education* is a powerful introduction to the principles of multicultural education. Its clear, descriptive format is an excellent tool for teachers trying to meet the challenges of racial, ethnic and cultural diversity. Gay describes the relationship between the principles of general education and multicultural education and explains how they are interrelated and complementary.

Kappa Delta Pi
P.O. Box A
Lafayette, IN 47906-0576
(800) 284-3167

In times of crisis, the classroom community may be the only stable element in a child's life. *The Crisis Manual for Early Childhood Teachers,* by Karen Miller, is an essential resource that describes how to handle the difficult problems of serious illness, divorce, racism, poverty and homelessness, among others. The book suggests ways to respond to each problem and provides guidance in knowing when and where to seek outside help for children and their families.

Gryphon House
P.O. Box 207
Beltsville, MD 20705
(800) 638-0928
Fax (301) 595-0051

Diversity in the Classroom, by Frances Kendall, is grounded in the premises that education is a powerful force in reducing "isms" and that teachers play critical roles as agents of change. Kendall's book is directed at 1) helping teachers identify their own biases and examine ways in which these biases may affect their teaching and 2) enabling educators to teach from a multicultural approach, regardless of the racial/ethnic makeup of their classes.

Teachers College Press
P.O. Box 20
Williston, VT 05495-0020
(800) 575-6566
Fax (802) 864-7626

The Inner World of the Immigrant Child gives readers insight into the fear, confusion and frustration young immigrants experience. Author Christina Igoa suggests ways to communicate with children — via drawing and storytelling — to understand their inner conflicts and to design interventions that address their social and psychological needs. She stresses the importance of recognizing and affirming children's own cultures while helping them make connections with the dominant culture of the classroom.

Lawrence Erlbaum Associates
10 Industrial Ave.
Mahwah, NJ 07430-2262
(800) 926-6579

Kids With Special Needs, by Veronica Getskow and Dee Konczal, is a comprehensive resource that familiarizes teachers, students and parents with various disabilities and health conditions, and explores ways to reduce children's fears about differences. Adept at helping readers handle sensitive subjects, the authors present questions that children — and adults — may ask about people with special needs. The book concludes with a useful "bibliotherapy" of resources organized by condition.

The Learning Works
P.O. Box 6187
Santa Barbara, CA 93160
(800) 235-5767

Looking In, Looking Out: Redefining Child Care and Early Education in a Diverse Society outlines five principles for childcare that fosters positive racial/ethnic identities in children and builds cross-cultural understanding. The authors include ideas for putting the principles into action and point out potential hurdles to implementation, as well as strategies for overcoming them. Self-reflective and pragmatic, this resource offers a comprehensive vision of quality childcare in our increasingly multiracial, multicultural and multilingual society.

California Tomorrow
Fort Mason Center, Bldg. B
San Francisco, CA 94123
(415) 441-7631
Fax (415) 441-7635

Vivian Gussin Paley, a classroom teacher for 37 years, received the Erikson Institute Award for Service to Children in 1987 and was named a MacArthur Fellow in 1989. In *Kwanzaa and Me*, Paley examines the impact of integration on young Black children. Throughout the book, the author has candid conversations with colleagues, parents and students which, in turn, lead to revelations about the experiences of minority children in our schools. Paley's other books include *White Teacher, Wally's Stories* and *You Can't Say You Can't Play*.

Harvard University Press
79 Garden St.
Cambridge, MA 02138
(800) 448-2242
Fax (800) 962-4983

If you can only buy one book for your classroom, consider the oversized color photo-and-text volume *Children Just Like Me*.

Photographer Barnabas Kindersley and teacher/author Anabel Kindersley spent two years visiting 30 countries to record the lives of children around the world. Each page is a stunning personal visit to a child's home. Information about environments, foods, toys, clothing and daily activities is as captivating as the smiles on the children's faces.

Dorling Kindersley
7800 Southland Blvd., Suite 200
Orlando, FL 32809
(800) 352-6651
Fax (800) 260-7658

Racial and Ethnic Diversity

Useful to classroom teachers, teacher educators and research scholars alike, these resources offer in-depth examinations of and multiple perspectives on issues related to racial and ethnic identity. Titles for adults will help educators better understand a pluralistic student population; children's titles will help foster an appreciation of cultural diversity both within the U.S. and around the world. (Note: Many of the books in Bookshelf Basics address cultural diversity.)

Culture in School Learning: Revealing the Deep Meaning, by Etta R. Hollins, is designed for pre-service teachers and can be used as a basic course text. This book contains foundational information on racial identity formation, culture and learning theory. Each chapter begins with focus questions and concludes with a summary and suggested learning activities.

Lawrence Erlbaum
10 Industrial Ave.
Mahwah, NJ 07430-2262
(800) 926-6579

Cross-Cultural Roots of Minority Child Development, edited by Patricia M. Greenfield and Rodney R. Cocking, examines the cultural heritage of diverse racial-ethnic minority groups. The contributing authors describe the cognitive strengths and learning preferences that children develop as a result of home child-rearing practices.

Lawrence Erlbaum
10 Industrial Ave.
Mahwah, NJ 07430-2262
(800) 926-6579

Early Childhood Education in American Indian and Alaska Native Communities, by Alice S. Paul, describes the history of forced assimilation through the U.S. government's Native schooling policies and offers a framework for effective contemporary early childhood programs serving Native children. Paul includes strategies for linking home and school learning, involving the community, maintaining Native language and training Native teachers.

ERIC Document Reproduction Service
7420 Fullerton Rd.
Springfield, VA 22153-2852
(800) 443-3742

Meeting the Challenge of Linguistic and Cultural Diversity in Early Childhood Education, edited by Eugene E. Garcia and Barry McLaughlin, is an invaluable resource for teachers dealing with bilingual and English as a Second Language instruction. The authors examine how preschool children acquire a second language and describe the developmental attributes that characterize children raised in multilingual environments.

Teachers College Press
P.O. Box 20
Williston, VT 05495-0020
(800) 575-6566
Fax (802) 864-7626

The Need for Story: Cultural Diversity in Classroom and Community, edited by Anne Haas Dyson and Celia Genishi, advocates the use of narrative to reflect children's diverse backgrounds and experiences. The contributors emphasize that storytelling is a form of power in the classroom. As such, it reveals complex relationships among the racial, ethnic and gender identities of students and teachers.

Teachers College Press
P.O. Box 20
Williston, VT 05495-0020
(800) 575-6566
Fax (802) 864-7626

Author Robyn M. Holmes spent six years in kindergarten classrooms studying *How Young Children Perceive Race.* Holmes interpreted children's words and drawings to determine their ideas about race and ethnicity and examined how these perceptions informed their self-concepts and social interactions.

Sage Publications
2455 Teller Rd.
Thousand Oaks, CA 91320
(805) 499-0721
Fax (805) 499-0871

Teaching and Learning in a Diverse World, by Patricia Ramsey, connects child development theory and research with multicultural education and provides examples of how to implement multicultural education in early learning settings. Ramsey also presents research and reflections concerning the ways in which teachers' behaviors and attitudes influence children.

Teachers College Press
P.O. Box 20
Williston, VT 05495-0020
(800) 575-6566
Fax (802) 864-7626

Children's Books

From the "whispering golds of late summer grasses" to "the roaring browns of bears and soaring eagles," children come in *All the*

Colors of the Earth. In lyric text and rich oil paintings, Sheila Hamanaka likens different skin colors and hair textures to things found in nature and, in the process, affirms the beauty of every child.

Morrow Junior Books
39 Plymouth St.
Fairfield, NJ 07004
(800) 843-9389

All the Colors We Are/Todos los Colores de Nuestra Piel, a bilingual book by Katie Kissinger, explains in simple language how we get our skin color. Photographs by Wernher Krutein present a rich array of skin hues.

Redleaf Press
450 N. Syndicate, Suite 5
St. Paul, MN 55104-4125
(800) 423-8309
Fax (800) 641-0115

W. Nikola-Lisa's *Bein' With You This Way* has an irresistible beat that is matched by Michael Bryant's exuberant oil crayon illustrations. The cast of characters enjoying fun and games in New York's Central Park have lots of differences, but they share the universal joy of friendship.

Publishers Group West
4065 Hollis St.
Emeryville, CA 94662
(800) 788-3123

Mary Ann Hoberman culled 15 poetic gems from different cultures to create *My Song Is Beautiful: Poems and Pictures in Many Voices.* Each poem is a celebration of self, told from the point of view of a child. Well-known children's artists used a range of techniques to make kaleidoscopic illustrations that reflect the diversity of the poets' voices.

Little, Brown and Co.
200 West St.
Waltham, MA 02154
(800) 759-0190
Fax (800) 286-9471

Four billion *People* on the planet, and each one is unique — so says Peter Spier in this picture book tribute to diversity. Spier crams his oversized illustrations with rich detail that illuminates all the glorious differences that make a world.

Doubleday
2451 S. Wolf Rd.
Des Plaines, IL 60018
(800) 323-9872

Ann Morris has written a series of books that explore the different ways in which people around the world meet the universal human needs of food, clothing, housing and love. Photos from every corner of the Earth accompany the simple text and foster a respect for difference. Titles in the series include: *Bread, Bread, Bread; Shoes, Shoes, Shoes; Houses and Homes;* and *Loving.*

Mulberry Books
39 Plymouth St.
Fairfield, NJ 07004
(800) 843-9389

Author Margy Burns Knight and illustrator Anne Sibley O'Brien have produced a book rich in family, tradition and color in *Welcoming Babies.* The book introduces us to families around the world as they celebrate the births of their children. Notes at the end of the book elaborate on the symbols and rituals of the celebrations. *Talking Walls* and *Who Belongs Here?* are two other books with multicultural themes that this collaborative team has produced.

Tilbury House Publishers
132 Water St.
Gardiner, ME 04345
(800) 582-1899
Fax (207) 582-8227

Families

The following books can assist early childhood educators in working harmoniously with families of varying compositions, backgrounds and value systems. These resources are also intended to promote in children an understanding of and appreciation for diverse family structures and other variable characteristics. (Note: Many of the books in Bookshelf Basics address family issues.)

Developing Cross-Cultural Competence: A Guide for Working With Young Children and Their Families examines the role culture plays in families' beliefs and provides strategies for cross-cultural interactions. Edited by Eleanor W. Lynch and Marci J. Hanson, the book supplies basic geographic, religious and linguistic background information on a plethora of U.S. cultures including European, Filipino, Middle Eastern and Pacific Islander.

Brookes Publishing
P.O. Box 10624
Baltimore, MD 21285-0624
(800) 638-3775
Fax (410) 337-8539

Author Laura Benkov examines the legal and social history of lesbian and gay parents in *Reinventing the Family*. Particularly helpful is a chapter focusing on the experiences of children of gay and lesbian parents as they face homophobia in their schools and communities.

Crown Publishers
400 Hahn Rd.
Westminster, MD 21157
(800) 726-0600
Fax (800) 659-2436

Family Ethnicity: Strength in Diversity explores the meaning of family ethnicity in relation to five major cultural groups in the U.S. — African American, Asian American, Latino, Muslim and Native American. Essays in this volume, edited by Harriette Pipes McAdoo, are by top scholars in the field and reflect multiple perspectives on issues such as assimilation, accommodation, poverty, isolation, inequality and discrimination.

Sage Publications
2455 Teller Rd.
Thousand Oaks, CA 91320
(805) 499-0721
Fax (805) 499-0871

Lisa Delpit's *Other People's Children: Cultural Conflict in the Classroom* is a collection of essays that explore what happens when the cultures of children of color collide with the mainstream culture of schools. Delpit explains how cultural background can influence a child's learning style and attitude toward teachers and suggests ways to consult with families to bridge cultural chasms.

W.W. Norton
800 Keystone Industrial Park
Scranton, PA 18512
(800) 233-4830
Fax (800) 458-6315

Roots and Wings: Affirming Culture in Early Childhood Programs, by Stacey York, is an excellent general reference on multicultural education that devotes a chapter to family influences. The author encourages educators to respect, without judging, parental values that differ from their own and to adopt a flexible teaching style that accommodates both teachers' and families' child-rearing beliefs.

Redleaf Press
450 N. Syndicate, Suite 5
St. Paul, MN 55104-4125
(800) 423-8309
Fax (800) 641-0115

Black, White, Other, by Lise Funderberg, explores the lives of adult children from black-white unions. Forty-six biracial individuals candidly tell their personal stories of love and marriage, raising children and facing racism.

William Morrow
39 Plymouth St.
Fairfield, NJ 07004
(800) 843-9389

Children's Books

Black is Brown is Tan is a story involving all the members of an interracial family. This lyric classic, written by poet Arnold Adoff and illustrated by Emily Arnold McCully, is one of many available from Great Owl Books' Butternut Collection, which was created especially for multiracial families. Other titles in the series include *Black, White, Just Right!* and *Real Sisters.*

Great Owl Books
33 Watchung Plaza
Montclair, NJ 07042-4111
(800) 299-3181
Fax (201) 783-5899

After a young boy's parents get a divorce, he discovers that *Daddy's Roommate* is fun to be with, just like Daddy. Written and illustrated by Michael Willhoite, the story affirms that being gay is "one more kind of love." Other books from the same publisher that feature gay and lesbian parents include *Heather Has Two Mommies, Gloria Goes to Gay Pride* and *Families.*

Alyson Wonderland
P.O. Box 4371
Los Angeles, CA 90078
(213) 871-1225

In *Dounia,* by Zidrou, a little girl travels to a different country to meet her adoptive parents and is happily overwhelmed by the unusual sights and sounds of her new home. Natacha Karvoskaia's soft, colorful drawings send a positive message about interracial adoption.

Kane/Miller Publishers
P.O. Box 310529
Brooklyn, NY 11231
(718) 624-5120

Mary Ann Hoberman pays homage to all kinds of families — adoptive, blended, extended and more — in *Fathers, Mothers, Sisters, Brothers: A Collection of Family Poems.* Her trademark rollicking rhymes, accompanied by Marylin Hafner's multicultural illustrations, proclaim that whether it's 10 members or two, a family is made up of people who love each other.

Little, Brown and Co.
200 West St.
Waltham, MA 02154
(800) 759-0190
Fax (800) 286-9471

Sanu, Eric and April all have a parent who was born outside of the U.S. — one in Senegal, one in Puerto Rico and one in China. Author/photographer Susan Kuklin helps each child tell us *How*

My Family Lives in America in this nonfiction book. Recipes for "the things we eat" are included.

Simon & Schuster
200 Old Tappan Rd.
Old Tappan, NJ 07675
(800) 223-2336
Fax (800) 445-6991

Mama, Do You Love Me? asks a young Inuit girl in this book by Barbara M. Joose. Artist Barbara Lavallee's vibrant Arctic scenes accent the mother's reassuring answer.

Chronicle Books
85 Second St.
San Francisco, CA 94105
(800) 722-6657
Fax (800) 858-7787

Two Lands, One Heart, by Jeremy Schmidt, is the true story of TJ's journey from Colorado to Vietnam, the country where his mother was born. Vivid photographs by Ted Wood let the reader glimpse the sights that greet TJ as he learns about the big city market, his grandfather's farm, silk worms and rice paddies.

Walker and Co.
435 Hudson St.
New York, NY 10014
(800) 289-2553
Fax (212) 727-0984

Organizations

The Clearinghouse for Immigrant Education (CHIME) is a toll-free hot line for information on foreign-born children, their parents and the public schools. CHIME staff members not only help

with problem-solving but offer reproductions of research, literature and teaching materials at a nominal cost.

Clearinghouse for Immigrant Education
100 Boylston St., Suite 737
Boston, MA 02116
(800) 441-7192

The Center for the Study of Biracial Children offers information
and resources related to interracial families. Training, consulta-
tion and articles that address how teachers can best serve the
needs of multiracial children are all available.

CSBC
2300 S. Krameria St.
Denver, CO
(303) 692-9008

Gender Equity

Following are resources to consult for help in avoiding the pitfalls of gender stereotyping and bias, and for ideas about introducing nontraditional role models in the early childhood classroom. (Note: Many of the books in Bookshelf Basics devote sections to gender equity.)

Vivian Gussin Paley's *Boys and Girls: Superheroes in the Doll Corner* explores how children investigate gender roles through classroom play. As Paley attempts to alter her kindergartners' stereotyped play patterns, she discovers and reflects on her own gender-based prejudices and how they impact her young charges.

University of Chicago Press
11030 S. Langley
Chicago, IL 60628
(800) 621-2736
Fax (800) 621-8476

Building Gender Fairness in Schools, by Beverly Stitt, gives teachers a thorough look at how gender bias is reinforced in schools and helps teachers identify their own biases in order to become better teachers.

Southern Illinois University Press
P.O. Box 3697
Carbondale, IL 62902-3697
(800) 346-2680
Fax (800) 346-2681

How can teachers create an early childhood environment that is "father friendly" and reach out to the community to welcome male classroom volunteers? James Levine offers ideas and inspiration in *Getting Men Involved: Strategies for Early Childhood*

Programs. Levine profiles model programs around the country and details the benefits of male involvement for children, families and teachers.

Scholastic
P.O. Box 7502
Jefferson City, MO 65102
(800) 325-6149

Perspectives on Non-Sexist Early Childhood Education takes a broad look at sex-role stereotyping. Edited by Barbara Sprung, the book also examines ways to pattern non-sexist roles and offers useful guidelines for the development of unbiased educational materials.

Teachers College Press
P.O. Box 20
Williston, VT 05495-0020
(800) 575-6566
Fax (802) 864-7626

Reading the Difference: Gender and Reading in Elementary Classrooms, edited by Myra Barrs and Sue Pidgeon, explores the relationship between reading and gender and presents model classrooms in which teachers are creating rich, inclusive reading environments. Twelve teachers and researchers contribute their experience in choosing books, working with beginning readers and drawing on parent resources to promote gender equity.

Stenhouse Publishers
P.O. Box 1929
Columbus, OH 43216-1929
(800) 988-9812
Fax (614) 487-2272

Children's Books

Amazing Grace, by Mary Hoffman, gives young children a model of independence in Grace, an African American girl who believes she can be anything she wants to be — even Peter Pan in the school play. Although some classmates argue that her race and gender preclude her playing the part, Grace remains undeterred. Paintings by Caroline Binch capture Grace's spirit.

Dial Books for Young Readers
120 Woodbine St.
Bergenfield, NJ 07621
(800) 253-6476

With *Daddies at Work* and *Mommies at Work,* Eve Merriam has produced two books that emphasize that anyone can do anything. Eugenie Fernandes' illustrations depict moms and dads busy at all kinds of jobs — from driving buses to painting portraits.

Simon & Schuster
200 Old Tappan Rd.
Old Tappan, NJ 07675
(800) 223-2336
Fax (800) 445-6791

Father Gander's Nursery Rhymes, written by Dr. Doug Larche and illustrated by Carolyn Marie Blattel, gives boys and girls equal time in rhyme. In these snappy retellings of traditional Mother Goose verses, "Jill-Be-Nimble" is every bit as agile as Jack, and "Larry, Larry Quite Contrary" enjoys tending the garden as much as Mary. The retooled rhymes retain all of their original music and charm.

Advocacy Press
P.O. Box 236
Santa Barbara, CA 93102
(800) 676-1480

The Girl Who Loved Caterpillars retells a story discovered on a 12th-century Japanese scroll. Author Jean Merrill and artist Floyd Cooper create a vivid portrait of Izumi, a free-spirited girl who refuses to give in to her society's strict notions of women's roles.

The Putnam & Grossett Group
One Grossett Dr.
Kirkwood, NY 13795
(800) 847-5515

The Paper Bag Princess, by Robert Munsch, turns the traditional fairy tale on its head as the brave and spirited title charater rescues a prince from an irksome dragon. The prince and princess part ways after the adventure, since a wedding isn't necessary to achieve "happily ever after" in this unconventional fairy tale. Pictures by Michael Martchenko bring the story to life.

Phoenix Learning Resources
2349 Chaffee Dr.
St. Louis, MO 63146
(800) 221-1274

William's Doll is the subject of concern among his brothers and father, who don't believe a doll is the proper toy for a boy. But William and his grandmother think differently, and they teach others to do the same. Charlotte Zolotow's text is sweetly complemented by William Pène Du Bois' illustrations.

HarperCollins
1000 Keystone Industrial Park
Scranton, PA 18512
(800) 242-7737
Fax (800) 822-4790

Willie's Not the Hugging Kind after a friend teases him for being affectionate. In this story written by Joyce D. Barrett and illustrated by Pat Cummings, Willie decides he's going to stop hugging his family — until he misses it so much that he finally reconciles his love for them with his desire to win his friend's approval.

Great Owl Books
33 Watchung Plaza
Montclair, NJ 07042-4111
(800) 299-3181
Fax (201) 783-5899

Ability Differences

These resources provide support for including children with special needs in the classroom community. They also suggest strategies for increasing awareness and acceptance of people with disabilities. (Note: See also Kids With Special Needs *in Bookshelf Basics.)*

Creating an Inclusive School, edited by Richard A. Villa and Jacqueline S. Thousand, offers an overview of the history of educating children with disabilities and presents compelling rationales for the inclusive classroom. Essays, which describe promising practices in K-12 schools, also put a human face on the issue by including reflections from parents and teachers of children who have been mainstreamed.

Association for Supervision and Curriculum Development
1250 N. Pitt St.
Alexandria, VA 22314
(800) 933-2723

Including All of Us: An Early Childhood Curriculum About Disability is a guidebook compiled by Project Inclusive that contains a trio of units about understanding disabilities. The units — all of which take into account gender and cultural issues — have been piloted successfully in preschool classrooms.

Educational Equity Concepts
114 E. 32nd St.
New York, NY 10016
(212) 725-1803

Pyllis A. Chandler addresses the questions and anxieties of teachers trying to create an inclusive classroom in *A Place for Me: Including Children With Special Needs in Early Care and*

Education. Geared toward teachers who have little or no experience working with children who have special needs, the book offers practical tips for promoting physical and social integration, as well as ideas about how to balance the needs of typical and exceptional children.

NAEYC
1509 16th St. N.W.
Washington, DC 20036-1426
(800) 424-2460

Read It Again! Books to Prepare Children for Inclusion, by Sharon Vaughn and Liz Rothlein, suggests 14 titles to foster understanding and acceptance of students with special needs. The guide includes thoughtful and sensitive discussion starters, as well as follow-up activities relating to each book.

Addison-Wesley
One Jacob Way
Redding, MA 01867
(800) 552-2259

Toward Inclusive Classrooms, by Mary Dalheim, focuses on how to create a classroom environment that successfully integrates students with special needs. Six innovative inclusion programs from elementary, middle and high schools across the country are described by the teachers who use them. The resource lists, reproducible pages and teaching tips offer guidance for practical application.

NEA Professional Library
P.O. Box 509
West Haven, CT 06516
(800) 229-4200

Children's Books

The Handmade Alphabet, by artist Laura Rankin, explores the visual world of signing. The manual is more than a practical tool for teaching youngsters how to sign; it is also a work of art that captures the beauty of this silent language.

Dial Books for Young Readers
375 Hudson St.
120 Woodbine St.
Bergenfield, NJ 07621
(800) 253-6476

Knots on a Counting Rope explores the relationship between a Native American man and his blind grandson. Each time the grandfather retells the story of the boy's birth and naming, he ties another knot on a rope to symbolize both the passage of time and the boy's growing self-confidence. Ted Rand's watercolors harmonize perfectly with the text by Bill Martin Jr. and John Archambault.

VHPS
175 Fifth Ave.
New York, NY 10010
(800) 288-2131
Fax (800) 321-9299

Someone Special, Just Like You, by Tricia Brown with photos by Fran Ortiz, is filled with fun pictures of children doing their favorite things. That all the children shown have a disability is incidental.

Gryphon House
P.O. Box 207
Beltsville, MD 20705
(800) 638-0928
Fax (301) 595-0051

The title character in *Stay Away from Simon!* is a mentally disabled boy who helps two children find their way home during a snowstorm. Set in 1830 in Martha's Vineyard, this chapter book by Carol and Donald Carrick is useful for helping children overcome their fears about people who seem "different."

Clarion Books
181 Ballardville St.
Wilmington, MA 01887-7050
(800) 225-3362

Through love and empathy, the artist-narrator in *Talking to Angels* learns to hear and appreciate her autistic sister's "sound of silence." Sparse text and simple, childlike art by Esther Watson convey the need to honor, respect and accept difference.

Harcourt Brace & Co.
6277 Sea Harbor Dr.
Orlando, FL 32887
(800) 543-1918

Organizations

The Clearinghouse on Disabilities and Gifted Education is a division of ERIC that acquires, indexes and distributes relevant professional literature and educational information on disabilities across all age groups.

ERIC Clearinghouse on Disabilities and Gifted Education
Council for Exceptional Children
1920 Association Dr.
Reston, VA 20191
(800) 328-0272

The Special Needs Project is a unique organization that maintains a diverse and thorough list of books, resources and organizations addressing the special needs of young children. The staff is helpful and highly knowledgeable about the topic.

Special Needs Project
3463 State St., Suite 282
Santa Barbara, CA 93105
(805) 683-9633
Fax (805) 962-5087

Getting Along

These resources are designed to promote harmony in the classroom, from helping children establish friendships to resolving conflicts peacefully. (Note: Many of the titles in Bookshelf Basics address classroom community-building and conflict resolution.)

In *Children as Peacemakers*, by Joan Baer et al., three teachers tell the story of how they developed a conflict resolution program at a small Canadian elementary school. Thanks to the peacemaking curriculum, the atmosphere at the school improved, and making peace — as well as respecting others — became a common goal.

Heinemann
361 Hanover St.
Portsmouth, NH 03801-3912
(800) 541-2086

Early Violence Prevention: Tools for Teachers of Young Children, edited by Ronald G. Slaby, describes practical ways to respond to children's aggression, encourage cooperation, and enhance empathy and social skills. By reviewing research and telling stories of classroom experiences, this book skillfully illustrates that children can be taught to become nonviolent problem-solvers.

NAEYC
1509 16th St. N.W.
Washington, DC 20036-1426
(800) 424-2460

Diane Levin's *Teaching Young Children in Violent Times: Building a Peaceable Classroom* addresses the challenges of teaching children who are bombarded with acts and images of violence. The author's lucid presentation of the issues — appreciating diversity, the negative impact of media, teaching conflict resolution — is paired with simple, effective ideas for creating a peaceable classroom. Levin clearly delineates developmental issues and takes them into consideration for all teaching suggestions.

Educators for Social Responsibility
23 Garden St.
Cambridge, MA 02138
(800) 370-2515
Fax (617) 864-5164

Ways We Want Our Class to Be: Class Meetings That Build Commitment to Kindness and Learning, a publication of The Child Development Project (CDP), provides a glimpse of the way school *can* be — when students use class meetings to establish their own rules, solve problems, set goals and develop a sense of community. Outlines of discussion and facilitation techniques supplement descriptions of class meetings. Another CDP resource for building community in the classroom is *Among Friends: Classrooms Where Caring and Learning Prevail.*

Developmental Studies Center
2000 Embarcadero, Suite 305
Oakland, CA 94606-5300
(800) 666-7270

Children's Books

Russell Hoban's classic *Best Friends for Frances* poses a formidable question: Can a sister be a best friend? Frances learns a few things about excluding others in this book of discovered and reconciled friendships. Lillian Hoban's charming illustrations are as timeless as the story's moral.

HarperCollins
1000 Keystone Industrial Park
Scranton, PA 18512
(800) 242-7737
Fax (800) 822-4790

When Kyra's family moves in next door, the neighbors are anything but welcoming. *Black Like Kyra, White Like Me,* written and illustrated by Judith Vigna, tells the story of a friendship between two girls that is strengthened by adversity.

Albert Whitman & Co.
6340 Oakton St.
Morton Grove, IL 60053
(800) 255-7675
Fax (847) 581-0039

In *Feathers and Fools,* by Mem Fox, swans and peacocks self-destruct in battle, leaving behind two eggs. These eggs hatch in the ruins, form an alliance for peace and harmony, and establish a trusting relationship. Muted acrylic paintings by Nicholas Wilton create a startling setting of destruction and reconciliation.

Harcourt Brace & Co.
6277 Sea Harbor Dr.
Orlando, FL 32887
(800) 543-1918

In the Leo Lionni fable *Frederick,* the title character's memories of summer colors sustain a group of mice through a hard winter. The story poignantly illustrates the importance of everyone's contribution to the community. *It's Mine!; Swimmy;* and *Tilly and the Wall* are three other Lionni fables that teach the respective values of sharing, cooperation and breaking down barriers.

Alfred A. Knopf
400 Hahn Rd.
Westminster, MD 21157
(800) 726-0600

In *The Hating Book,* written by Charlotte Zolotow with pictures by Ben Schecter, a simple miscommunication between friends leads to hurt feelings and angry words. The story is useful in helping young children understand that there are two sides to every conflict.

HarperCollins
1000 Keystone Industrial Park
Scranton, PA 18512
(800) 242-7737
Fax (800) 822-4790

Smoky Night, by Eve Bunting, tells the fictional story of a young African American boy who overcomes cultural differences and reaches out to his Asian neighbor during the 1992 Los Angeles riots. Bold paintings and mixed-media collages by David Diaz accompany the text.

Harcourt Brace & Co.
6377 Sea Harbor Dr.
Orlando, FL 32887
(800) 543-1918

Organizations

The Peace Education Foundation, whose program was implemented by educators at North Miami Elementary School *(see Chapter 6)*, offers a variety of teaching tools to help children become peacemakers. One resource developed especially for young children is *Peacemaking Skills for Little Kids,* an activity booklet that explains the basic tenets of friendship, community and responsibility. The foundation also sponsors an early childhood institute on building a peaceful school community.

Peace Education Foundation
P.O. Box 191153
1900 Biscayne Blvd.
Miami, FL 33132
(800) 749-8838

Educators for Social Responsibility provides a wide range of educational support for conflict resolution, including workshops, curricula, training manuals, activity books, brochures and reproducible readings.

Educators for Social Responsibility
School Conflict Resolution Programs
23 Garden St.
Cambridge, MA 02138
(617) 492-1764

Dealing With Feelings

The following resources offer guidance in helping children understand and express their emotions. They also address how to cope with a variety of stresses, including family problems, illness, violence and death, and how to support children's emotional healing. (Note: See also The Crisis Manual for Early Childhood Teachers *and* The Inner World of the Immigrant Child *in Bookshelf Basics.)*

Bad Guys Don't Have Birthdays, by Vivian Gussin Paley, explores how children work through their fears during fantasy play and storytelling. Paley's close observations of children's play enable her to discern their deepest concerns and support play as an intuitive coping strategy.

University of Chicago Press
11030 S. Langley
Chicago, IL 60628
(800) 621-2736
Fax (800) 621-8476

Reducing Stress in Young Children's Lives remains one of the most thorough discussions of stresses children face in both daily and extreme forms. The authors address — among other subjects — divorce, child abuse and sex education with realism, insight and sensitivity. A table highlighting the manifestations of stress is especially helpful for learning to recognize and respond to tell-tale signs of difficulties.

NAEYC
1509 16th St. N.W.
Washington, DC 20036-1426
(800) 424-2460

Children in Danger: Coping with the Consequences of Community Violence, by James Garbarino et al., deals with the issue of chronic violence and its impact on child development. Chapters address the school as a refuge and the use of art and play in the healing process.

Jossey-Bass
350 Sansome St.
San Francisco, CA 94104
(415) 433-1740

Edited by Janet Brown McCracken and first published in 1979, *Unsmiling Faces: How Preschools Can Heal,* edited by Lesley Koplow, creates a framework for paying attention to and addressing the emotional lives of preschool children. Practical child psychology is integrated into curriculum development, therapeutic activities and evaluations of adult/child relationships.

Teachers College Press
P.O. Box 20
Williston, VT 05495-0020
(800) 575-6566
Fax (802) 864-7626

Richard Weissbourd challenges conventional assumptions about what factors put children at risk in *The Vulnerable Child.* The book helps the reader move beyond stereotypes about poverty, single parenthood and racial background to consider the broad range of problems — including chronic stress and depression — that can undermine parents and, consequently, their children.

Addison-Wesley
One Jacob Way
Reading, MA 01867
(800) 552-2259

Children's Books

A young immigrant from Vietnam tries hard to be the sweet and brave *Angel Child, Dragon Child* that her mother wants her to be, but the stresses of adapting to a new school in a new country make it difficult. Author Michele Maria Surat and illustrator Vo Dinh Mai sensitively chronicle the little girl's struggle to fit in.

Scholastic
P.O. Box 7502
Jefferson City, MO 65102
(800) 325-6149

Candid and poignant black-and-white photographs capture the tender relationship between tennis great Arthur Ashe, who died of AIDS in 1993, and his daughter, Camera, in *Daddy and Me.* The photos, taken by acclaimed photographer Jeanne Moutoussamy-Ashe (Camera's mom) and accompanied by Camera's own words, provide a simple but meaningful way to discuss AIDS with young children.

Random House
400 Hahn Rd.
Westminster, MD 21557
(800) 726-0600

Charles E. Avery's *Everybody Has Feelings/Todos Tenemos Sentimientos* is a bilingual portrait gallery of feelings, illustrated with black-and-white photos of children. The book is a good prelude to preschool and kindergarten discussions about similarities among people.

Open Hand Publishing
P.O. Box 22048
Seattle, WA 98122
(206) 323-2187

Feelings, by Aliki, is just right for children who are learning to recognize and articulate their emotions. The feelings described run the gamut from pure happiness to jealousy to love. *The Two of Them,* also by Aliki, describes the special relationship a little girl has with her grandfather and her deep feelings of love and loss when he dies.

Mulberry Books
39 Plymouth St.
Fairfield, NJ 07004
(800) 843-9389

Sachiko Means Happiness, but Sachiko doesn't feel very happy. Her grandmother — for whom Sachiko is named — has Alzheimer's and doesn't even recognize her. Sachiko is hurt and angry until the two go for a walk and she sees her namesake in a new light. Author Kimiko Sakai and illustrater Tomie Arai address a difficult issue with clarity and compassion.

Children's Book Press
246 First Ave., Suite 101
San Francisco, CA 94105
(415) 995-2200

A little girl's orderly world is upset when her mother takes a job outside the home in Marge Blaine's *The Terrible Thing That Happened at Our House.* But together, her family come up with some coping strategies that help the stressed-out narrator realize "the terrible thing" isn't so bad after all. Energetic watercolors by Hohn C. Wallace add to the humor.

Scholastic
P.O. Box 7502
Jefferson City, MO 65102
(800) 325-6149

In Judith Viorst's *The Tenth Good Thing About Barney*, a small boy struggles to think of 10 good things about his recently deceased cat. At first he can only think of nine things, but when he realizes the 10th he begins to understand — and accept — his cat's death. Erik Blegvad's pencil sketches evoke the boy's tender feelings for his beloved pet. By the same author, the book *Alexander and the Terrible, Horrible, No Good, Very Bad Day* takes a humorous look at everyday stresses in a child's life.

Aladdin Books
866 Third Ave.
New York, NY 10022
(800) 257-8247

Developing Values

These resources address how children understand and acquire values — from self-respect to social justice — and consider the impact of factors such as family, school and the media on moral development.

In *The Caring Child,* Nancy Eisenberg considers children's capacities for prosocial behavior. Eisenberg examines the forces that influence a child's moral growth and points out ways that parents and educators can cultivate kindness and compassion in children.

Harvard University Press
79 Garden St.
Cambridge, MA 02138
(800) 448-2242
Fax (800) 962-4983

Promoting Social and Moral Development in Young Children, by Carolyn Pope Edwards, presents research and theory about young children's emerging concepts of self and others, society and morality. The author suggests developmentally appropriate activities — including perspective-taking and causal reasoning — for supporting and guiding children as they form moral judgments.

Teachers College Press
P.O. Box 20
Williston, VT 05495-0020
(800) 575-6566
Fax (802) 864-7626

In *The Moral Life of Children,* Robert Coles investigates the struggle children undergo in understanding and expressing moral choices. His exploration takes him through a myriad of children's artwork and stories, and into their minds as they wrestle with movies, stories and myths. Cole's probing psychoanalysis of children's moral development is interspersed with (and supported by) scenarios in which children speak for themselves about their feelings, questions and deeds.

Houghton Mifflin
1900 S. Batavia Ave.
Geneva, IL 60134
(800) 225-3362
Fax (800) 634-7575

The Smart Parent's Guide to Kids' TV presents television as an enormously influential medium, with powers to do both good and evil. This highly readable book by Milton Chen offers tips for regulating TV consumption and fostering intelligent and critical viewing.

KQED Books and Tapes
5980 Miami Lakes Drive
Miami Lakes, FL 33014
(800) 358-3000

Sara Bullard's *Teaching Tolerance: Raising Open-Minded, Empathetic Children* helps parents and caregivers understand how children learn prejudice and how they can be guided toward tolerance. The book balances theory and reflection with practical advice and an extensive list of resources.

Doubleday
1540 Broadway
New York, NY 10036
(800) 223-6834

Children's Books
Eloise Greenfield's *Honey, I Love* is a classic book of poetry about

the simple things in life — as voiced by a child. The illustrations, by Diane and Leo Dillon, take us into the world of a young African American girl as she describes what she values most: family, friends and her own unique self.

HarperCollins
1000 Keystone Industrial Park
Scranton, PA 18512
(800) 242-7737
Fax (800) 822-4790

A caring elephant risks ridicule and rejection to rescue a community inhabiting a dust speck in the Dr. Seuss classic *Horton Hears a Who*. Horton offers a moral precept ("a person's a person, no matter how small") that little children can relate to. Other Seuss classics that consider moral matters — from environmental issues to prejudice to world peace — include *The Lorax, The Sneetches* and *The Butter Battle Book*.

Random House
400 Hahn Rd.
Westminster, MD 21557
(800) 726-0600
Fax (800) 659-2436

On the Day You Were Born, the Earth celebrated in all its glory. Debra Frasier's exquisite paper collages illustrate the many ways in which the natural world welcomes a newborn baby in this esteem-boosting tribute to all children.

Harcourt Brace & Co.
6277 Sea Harbor Dr.
Orlando, FL 32887
(800) 543-1918

This Is Our House, by Michael Rosen, tells the story of George, who does not allow girls, twins, short people or children with glasses into his cardboard abode. But when his peers turn the tables by excluding people with red hair from their play, carrot-topped George learns a lesson about making everybody feel welcome. Children will love Bob Graham's witty illustrations.

Candlewick Press
120 Woodbine St.
Bergenfield, NJ 07621
(800) 227-9604

Stereotypes come under scrutiny in the book *Paul and Sebastian,* written by René Escudié and illustrated by Ulises Wensell. Parents refuse to allow their sons to play together because one lives in an apartment and the other in a trailer, until a minor crisis makes them realize they have more in common than they thought.

Kane/Miller Book Publishers
P.O. Box 310529
Brooklyn, NY 11231-0529
(718) 624-5120

Organizations

The Anti-Defamation League offers educational outreach programs and publications aimed at prejudice awareness/reduction relating to race, ethnicity, disability, gender, religion and other issues. *Teacher, they called me a _____!* is an anti-bias activity book geared toward elementary-aged children.

Anti-Defamation League of B'nai B'rith
823 United Nations Plaza
New York, NY 10017
(212) 490-2525

The human rights organization Amnesty International produces materials designed to promote intercultural understanding and a commitment to justice. Among the resources it provides are the book *Human Rights for Children,* which helps kids ages 3 to 12 develop an awareness of their own rights and the rights of others, and *The Universal Declaration of Human Rights,* a 20-minute video that portrays the 30 articles of this document in an innovative animated form.

Amnesty International
322 Eighth Ave.
New York, NY 10001
(212) 807-8400

Texts of the Universal Declaration of Human Rights and the Convention on the Rights of the Child, as well as a variety of posters, books and lesson plans, are available from the United Nations.

U.N. Publications
2 United Nations Plaza
Room DC2-853
New York, NY 10017
(800) 253-9646

Hands, Ears and Eyes On

The following activity books, art materials, posters, puppets, dolls, songbooks and other items can help you create an environment and curriculum that celebrate diversity and foster caring and unity among young children.

Activity Books and Curricula

The Best Self-Esteem Activities for the Elementary Grades offers an excellent overview of the theory behind self-esteem and emotion management for children, as well as strategies for promoting children's sense of personal agency and self-fulfillment. By the same publisher, the book *Everybody Wins!* includes 100 games that focus on inclusion, cooperation and cross-cultural interaction.

Innerchoice Publishing
P.O. Box 2476
Spring Valley, CA 91979
(619) 698-2437
Fax (619) 698-3348

Feeling Strong, Feeling Free provides dozens of activities that allow children to explore the joys of movement and enhance feelings of trust and togetherness in the classroom.

NAEYC
1509 16th St. N.W.
Washington, DC 20036-1462
(800) 424-2460

First Time, Circle Time: Shared Group Experiences for Three-, Four- and Five-Year-Olds abounds with song lyrics, reading, art and movement suggestions designed to bring (and keep) children together at Circle Time.

Globe/Fearon Educational Publishers
P.O. Box 2649
Columbus, OH 43216
(800) 848-9500
Fax (614) 771-7361

Need an idea for a multicultural project? This appealing trio of activity books can help: *Hands Around the World: 365 Ways to Build Cultural Awareness and Global Respect; The Kids' Multicultural Art Book;* and *The Kids' Multicultural Cookbook.* Unlike many other activity books, these provide important background information about suggested projects.

Williamson Publishing Co.
P.O. Box 185
Charlotte, VT 05445
(800) 234-8791

Learning the Skills of Peacemaking includes 56 lesson plans for teaching "peace skills." The book emphasizes the responsibility of individuals in promoting peace, a theme that is reinforced with creative activities and insightful discussion guidelines.

Jalmar Press
24426 S. Main St., Suite 702
Carson, CA 90745
(800) 662-9622
Fax (310) 816-3092

Making It Better: Activities for Children Living in a Stressful World offers art, play and storytelling activities to promote healing and recovery in children who are experiencing upset or trauma. Activities are supported by background information describing how children cope with loss.

Redleaf Press
450 N. Syndicate, Suite 5
St. Paul, MN 55104-4125
(800) 423-8309
Fax (800) 641-0115

The *Multicultural Game Book* brings together more than 70 games from 30 countries for children ages 6 and up. The book includes background information as well as extension activities.

Scholastic
P.O. Box 7502
Jefferson City, MO 65102
(800) 325-6149

More than 160 preschool activities that revolve around feelings, respect, encouragement and negotiation can be found in *The Peaceful Classroom.*

Gryphon House
P.O. Box 207
Beltsville, MD 20705
(800) 638-0928
Fax (301) 595-0051

Ready to Use Multicultural Activities for Primary Children divides its riches into three parts — self-esteem, mutual respect and multicultural contributions. Activities are printed on reproducible pages and preceded by discussion guidelines and annotated "literature connection" suggestions.

The People's Publishing Group
P.O. Box 70
Rochelle Park, NJ 07662
(800) 822-1080

The first volume of *Thinking, Feeling, Behaving: An Emotional Education Curriculum for Children,* by Ann Vernon, is a compendium of classroom activities based on the principle that thinking things through rationally is one of the best ways to overcome problems. The activities focus on developing children's emotional intelligence.

Research Press
1612 N. Mattis Ave.
Champaign, IL 61821
(217) 352-3273

Words Can Hurt You, a book which features dozens of anti-bias activities, will help teachers infuse tolerance themes throughout the curriculum.

Addison-Wesley
One Jacob Way
Reading, MA 01867
(800) 552-2259

Posters and Displays
Flowers of One Garden is a beautiful poster designed to promote unity among people from different ethnic and racial backgrounds. A teaching guide that includes tips for using the poster, as well as additional resources, accompanies the artwork.

Sharon Firooz
749 S. Lemay, Suite A3-319
Fort Collins, CO 80524
(970) 226-2059

The Family Diversity Project offers traveling photo and text exhibits that highlight the joys of diverse families. *Love Makes a*

Family features interviews with and images of families that include lesbian or gay youth, parents or grandparents. More than 30 multiracial families were interviewed and photographed for the exhibit *Of Many Colors*. For more information, or to arrange an exhibition in your school, contact:

Love Makes a Family	Of Many Colors
P.O. Box 1209	P.O. Box 1493
Amherst, MA 01004-1209	Kingston, PA 18704
(413) 256-0502	(717) 331-3336
Fax (413) 253-3977	Fax (717) 331-3337

People of the World is a vibrant 8-foot-long poster crammed with facts and illustrations celebrating human diversity.

Anatomical Chart Co.
8221 Kimball Ave.
Skokie, IL 60076
(800) 621-7500

A unique interfaith calendar describes a variety of religions, including their fundamental principles and the significance of various icons and shrines. The calendar records holy days for Anglican, Baha'i, Buddhist, Catholic, Hindu, Islamic, Jewish, Native American, Orthodox Christian, Protestant, Sikh and Zoroastrian religions.

The National Conference
360 N. Michigan, Suite 1009
Chicago, IL 60601
(312) 236-9272

The Getty Center for Education in the Arts presents four different sets of multicultural art prints to help students gain a deeper understanding of the way art reflects cultural values. The large laminated prints depict African American, Asian-Pacific, Mexican

American and Native American art. Discussion questions and art activities are printed on the back of each full-color reproduction.

Crystal Productions
P.O. Box 2159
Glenview, IL 60025
(800) 255-8629

Stick Up For Yourself is a colorful poster that offers tips for building personal power and self-esteem.

Free Spirit Publishing
400 First Ave. N., Suite 616
Minneapolis, MN 55401
(800) 735-7323

Music

Children of the World and *Joining Hands With Other Lands* are just two of many fine recordings available from Kimbo Educational. Recordings are accompanied by lyrics and activity suggestions.

Kimbo Educational
P.O. Box 477
Long Branch, NJ 07740
(800) 631-2187

World Music Press offers an international selection of recordings. Books accompanying the recordings include maps, pictures and study guides related to the featured country and provide cultural, historical and musical background information.

World Music Press
P.O. Box 2565
Danbury, CT 06813-2565
(203) 748-1131

Songs for Peacemakers is a teaching kit that offers ideas and resources for using music as a tool in conflict resolution. The kit includes an audio cassette, video, teacher's handbook and reproducible masters. The cassette and lyrics can also be purchased separately from the kit.

Educational Activities
P.O. Box 392
Freeport, NY 11520
(800) 79-PEACE

Dolls and Puppets
Looking for hand puppets that realistically represent children of different racial and ethnic heritages? Fire Robin Puppets offers teachers of young children a selection of four such puppets, all handmade: an Asian boy, an African American boy, a European American girl and a Native American girl.

Fire Robin Puppets
Bridge Street, Box 1007
Richmond, VT 05477
(800) 235-5013

Children delight in soft, machine-washable "Treehuggers" dolls and often exclaim, "They look like me!" African American, East Asian, South Asian, European American and Native American are available. All come with removable clothing and real shoelaces.

Great Owl Books
33 Watchung Plaza
Montclair, NJ 07042-4111
(800) 299-3181
Fax (201) 783-5899

contributors

Sara Bullard (Chapter 6) was founding director of the Teaching Tolerance project. She is the author of *Free at Last: A History of the Civil Rights Movement and Those Who Died in the Struggle* (Oxford) and *Teaching Tolerance: Raising Open-Minded, Empathetic Children* (Doubleday).

Jim Carnes (chapters 1, 2, 4, 5 [in part] and 7, Reflections 12 and 14 [in part]) is director of the Teaching Tolerance project and author of *Us and Them: A History of Intolerance in America* (Oxford). He was previously an associate editor at *Encyclopaedia Britannica*.

Marie Hofer (Chapter 3) is a free-lance writer based in Knoxville, Tenn. In addition to her work for *Teaching Tolerance* magazine, she has has contributed to the "Big Picture" poster project and currently develops on-line educational services.

Vivian Gussin Paley (Foreword) taught young children for 37 years in New Orleans, New York and Chicago. Her widely acclaimed books include *White Teacher; You Can't Say You Can't Play; Kwanzaa and Me;* and, most recently, *The Girl with the Brown Crayon* (all Harvard). She received the Erikson Institute Award for Children in 1987 and was named a MacArthur Fellow in 1989.

Nancy Polk (Chapter 5, in part) is a free-lance writer based in Woodbridge, Conn. She has covered education issues for *The New York Times* for 30 years and has written and edited for a variety of publications, including *Columbia Journalism Review, Chicago Tribune* and *Toronto Star.*

Rosa Hernández Sheets (Reflections and Applications 1-11 and 13, Application 12 and Reflection 14 [in part]) was the 1996-97 Teaching Tolerance Research Fellow. She is senior editor of *Racial and Ethnic Identity in School Practices: Aspects of Human Development* (Lawrence Erlbaum) and has published articles in *The Urban Review, Social Education* and *The Americas Review,* among other journals. ★